Congaree National Park Visitor Study

Winter 2012

Natural Resource Report NPS/NRSS/EQD/NRR— 2012/608

Cynthia Jette, Yen Le, Steven J. Hollenhorst

Visitor Services Project
Park Studies Unit
University of Idaho
Moscow, ID 83844-1139

December 2012

U.S. Department of the Interior
National Park Service
Natural Resource Stewardship and Science
Fort Collins, Colorado

The National Park Service, Natural Resource Stewardship and Science office in Fort Collins, Colorado, publishes a range of reports that address natural resource topics. These reports are of interest and applicability to a broad audience in the National Park Service and others in natural resource management, including scientists, conservation and environmental constituencies, and the public.

The Natural Resource Report Series is used to disseminate high-priority, current natural resource management information with managerial application. The series targets a general, diverse audience, and may contain NPS policy considerations or address sensitive issues of management applicability.

All manuscripts in the series receive the appropriate level of peer review to ensure that the information is scientifically credible, technically accurate, appropriately written for the intended audience, and designed and published in a professional manner.

Data in this report were collected and analyzed using methods based on established, peer-reviewed protocols and were analyzed and interpreted within the guidelines of the protocols.

Views, statements, findings, conclusions, recommendations, and data in this report do not necessarily reflect views and policies of the National Park Service, U.S. Department of the Interior. Mention of trade names or commercial products does not constitute endorsement or recommendation for use by the U.S. Government.

This report is available from the Social Science Division (http://www.nature.nps.gov/socialscience/index.cfm) and the Natural Resource Publications Management website (http://www.nature.nps.gov/publications/nrpm/).

This report and other reports by the Visitor Services Project (VSP) are available from the VSP website (http://www.psu.uidaho.edu/c5/vsp/vsp-reports/) or by contacting the VSP office at (208) 885-7863.

Please cite this publication as:

Jette, C., Y. Le, and S. J. Hollenhorst. 2012. Congaree National Park visitor study: Winter 2012. Natural Resource Report NPS/NRSS/EQD/NRR—2012/608. National Park Service, Fort Collins, Colorado.

NPS 178/119309, December 2012

Contents

Contents (continued)

Executive Summary

This visitor study report profiles a systematic random sample of Congaree National Park (NP) visitors during January 27- March 7, 2012. A total of 446 questionnaires were distributed to visitor groups. Of those, 341 questionnaires were returned, resulting in a 76.5% response rate.

Group size and type
Fifty-five percent of visitor groups consisted of two people. Fifty-eight percent of visitor groups consisted of family groups.

State or country of residence
United States visitors were from 34 states and comprised 98% of total visitation during the survey period, with 52% from South Carolina. International visitors were from 7 countries.

Frequency of visits
Seventy-eight percent of visitors visited the park once in the past 12 months and 63% were visiting the park for the first time in their lives. Nineteen percent had visited four or more times in their lifetime.

Age, ethnicity, race, and educational level
Forty-seven percent of visitors were ages 51-70 years, 22% were 21-40 years old, 12% were ages 15 years or younger. One percent were Hispanic or Latino. Most visitors (94%) were White, 3% were Asian and 2% were African American. Thirty-nine percent of respondents had a graduate degree and 38% had completed a bachelor's degree.

Physical conditions
Six percent of visitor groups had members with physical conditions affecting their ability to access or participate in activities and services.

Awareness of park programs
Sixty-five percent of visitor groups were aware, prior to their visit, of the various programs offered at the park.

Knowledge of wilderness
Fifty-nine percent of respondents indicated they were aware of what congressionally designated wilderness is before their visit to the park. Forty-three percent of visitor groups said they learned about wilderness while at the park.

Non-native species management
Fifty percent of respondents were aware of the policy regarding removal of non-native species. Most visitor groups (86%) were in support of removal of non-native plants and 77% were supportive of removal of non-native animals.

Scientific research and education in the park
Forty-seven percent of visitor groups noticed scientists working or scientific markers or equipment being used in the park. Through programs or products, 26% of the visitors learned about the results of scientific studies conducted at the park.

Information sources
Most visitors (94%) obtained information about the park prior to their visit. Of those visitors, 56% used the park website and 30% obtained their information from friends/relatives/word of mouth.

Park as destination
Seventy-five percent of visitor groups said the park was their primary destination and 21% said it was one of several destinations.

Primary reason for visiting the area
Twenty-eight percent of visitor groups were residents of the area (within 1-hour drive of the park). The most common primary reason for visiting the park area among nonresident visitor groups was to visit the park (65%).

Executive Summary (continued)

Overnight stays　　Thirty-eight percent of visitor groups stayed overnight away from home either in the park or the area. Of those visitors that stayed outside the park (within a 1-hour drive), 49% stayed one night and 23% stayed two nights.

Accommodations　　Of those visitor groups that stayed outside the park (within 1-hour drive), 82% stayed in a lodge, hotel, motel, cabin, rented condo/home, or B&B.

Time spent at park and in the area　　The average length of stay in the park was 8.8 hours or 0.4 days. The average length of stay in the area was 31.4 hours, or 1.3 days.

Activities　　The most common visitor activities within the park were walking/hiking (85%), visiting the visitor center (71%), and birdwatching (25%).

Use of park trails　　The Elevated Boardwalk Trail was used by 79% of visitor groups and the Low Boardwalk Trail was used by 70%.

Information services and facilities　　The information services and facilities most commonly used by visitor groups were park brochure/map (90%), assistance from park staff (83%), and visitor center exhibits (75%).

Visitor services and facilities　　The visitor services and facilities most commonly used by visitor groups were boardwalks (89%), restrooms (88%), and parking areas (85%).

Protecting park attributes, resources, and experiences　　The highest combined proportions of "extremely important" and "very important" ratings of protecting park attributes, resources, and experiences included clean air (94%), natural quiet/sounds of nature (94%), and clean water (93%).

Elements affecting park experience　　Thirty-nine percent of visitor groups reported that encountering small numbers of visitors on the trails added to their trip experiences. Airplane noise detracted from 42% of the visitor groups' experiences.

Expenditures　　The average visitor group expenditure (inside and outside the park within a 1-hour drive) was $153. The median group expenditure (50% of groups spent more and 50% of groups spent less) was $55. The average total expenditure per capita was $74.

Future visit　　Sixty-eight percent of visitor groups were interested in canoeing/kayaking on future visits and 57% were interested in either owl prowls or night walk/night sky programs. Seventy-four percent of visitor groups were interested in learning more about plants and animals on future visits and 61% were interested in learning more about either champion trees or old growth floodplain forest.

Overall quality　　Most visitor groups (97%) rated the overall quality of facilities, services, and recreational opportunities at Congaree NP as "very good" or "good." No visitor groups rated the overall quality as "very poor."

For more information about the Visitor Services Project, please contact the Park Studies Unit at the University of Idaho at (208) 885-7863 or the following website http://www.psu.uidaho.edu.

Acknowledgements

We thank Cynthia Jette for compiling the report, Lauren Gurniewicz for overseeing the fieldwork, the staff and volunteers of Congaree NP for assisting with the survey, and David Vollmer and Matthew Strawn for data processing.

About the Authors

Cynthia Jette is a research assistant for the Visitor Services Project at the University of Idaho. Yen Le, Ph.D., is Assistant Director of the Visitor Services Project at the University of Idaho, and Steven Hollenhorst, Ph.D., was the Director of the Park Studies Unit, Department of Conservation Social Sciences, University of Idaho.

Introduction

This report describes the results of a visitor study at Congaree National Park (NP) in Hopkins, SC, conducted January 27 – March 7, 2012 by the National Park Service (NPS) Visitor Services Project (VSP), part of the Park Studies Unit (PSU) at the University of Idaho.

As described in the National Park Service website for Congaree National Park: "Welcome to the largest remnant of old-growth floodplain forest remaining on the continent! Experience champion trees, towering to record size amidst astonishing biodiversity…Congaree National Park houses a museum quality exhibit area within the Harry Hampton Visitor Center, a 2.4 mile boardwalk loop trail, over 20 miles of backwoods hiking trails, canoeing, kayaking, fishing and more…As a designated Wilderness area, International Biosphere Reserve, Globally Important Bird Area, and the largest intact tract of old-growth floodplain forest in North America, Congaree National Park is home to a variety of ongoing research and education projects." (http://www.nps.gov/cong/index.htm, retrieved October, 2011).

Organization of the Report

This report is organized into three sections.

Section 1: **Methods**
This section discusses the procedures, limitations, and special conditions that may affect the study results.

Section 2: **Results**
This section provides a summary for each question in the questionnaire and includes visitor comments to open-ended questions. The presentation of the results of this study does not follow the order of questions in the questionnaire.

Section 3: **Appendices**
Appendix 1: *The Questionnaire*. A copy of the questionnaire distributed to visitor groups.

Appendix 2: *Additional Analysis.* A list of sample questions for cross-references and cross comparisons. Comparisons can be analyzed within a park or between parks. Results of additional analyses are not included in this report.

Appendix 3: *Decision Rules for Checking Nonresponse Bias.* An explanation of how the nonresponse bias was determined.

Presentation of the Results

Results are represented in the form of graphs (see Example 1 below), scatter plots, pie charts, tables, and text.

Key

1. The figure title describes the graph's information.

2. Listed above the graph, the "N" shows the number of individuals or visitor groups responding to the question. If "N" is less than 30, "**CAUTION!**" is shown on the graph to indicate the results may be unreliable.

5. appears when the total percentages do not equal 100 due to rounding.

** appears when total percentages do not equal 100 because visitors could select more than one answer choice.

3. Vertical information describes the response categories.

4. Horizontal information shows the number or proportion of responses in each category.

5. In most graphs, percentages provide additional information.

Example 1

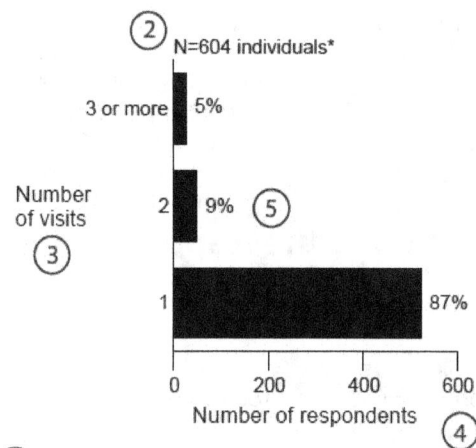

Figure 14. Number of visits to the park in past 12 months

Methods

Survey Design and Procedures

Sample size and sampling plan

All VSP questionnaires follow design principles outlined in Don A. Dillman's book *Mail and Internet Surveys: The Tailored Design Method* (2007). Using this method, the sample size was calculated based on park visitation statistics of previous years.

Brief interviews were conducted with a systematic, random sample of visitor groups that arrived at the visitor center during January 27 – March 7, 2012. Visitors were surveyed between the hours of 8 a.m. and 5 p.m. During this survey, 460 visitor groups were contacted and 446 of these groups (97%) accepted questionnaires. (The average acceptance rate for 250 VSP visitor studies conducted from 1988 through 2011 is 91.5%.) Questionnaires were completed and returned by 341 respondents, resulting in a 76.5% response rate for this study. (The average response rate for the 250 VSP visitor studies is 72.3%).

Questionnaire design

The Congaree NP questionnaire was developed at a workshop held with park staff to design and prioritize questions. Some of the questions were comparable with VSP studies conducted at other parks while others were customized for Congaree NP. Many questions asked visitors to choose answers from a list of responses, often with an open-ended option, while others were completely open-ended.

No pilot study was conducted to test the Congaree NP questionnaire. However, all questions followed Office Management and Budget (OMB) guidelines and/or were used in previous surveys; thus, the clarity and consistency of the survey instrument have been tested and supported.

Survey procedure

Visitor groups were greeted, briefly introduced to the purpose of the study, and asked to participate. If visitors agreed, they were asked which member (at least 16 years old) had the next birthday. The individual with the next birthday was selected to complete the questionnaire for the group. An interview, lasting approximately two minutes, was conducted with that person to determine group size, group type, age of the member completing the questionnaire, and how this visit to the park fit into their group's travel plans. These individuals were asked their names, addresses, and telephone numbers or email addresses in order to mail a reminder/thank-you postcard and follow-ups. Participants were asked to complete the questionnaire after their visit, and return it in the Business Reply Mail envelope provided.

Two weeks following the survey, a reminder/thank-you postcard was mailed to all participants who provided a valid mailing address (see Table 1). Replacement questionnaires were mailed to participants who had not returned their questionnaires four weeks after the survey. Seven weeks after the survey, a second round of replacement questionnaires was mailed to participants who had not returned their questionnaires.

Table 1. Follow-up mailing distribution

Round 1 Mailing	Date	U.S.	International	Total
Postcards	February 27, 2012	215	1	216
1st replacement	March 12, 2012	99	0	99
2nd replacement	April 2, 2012	68	0	68

Round 2 Mailing	Date	U.S.	International	Total
Postcards	March 9, 2012	124	2	126
1st replacement	March 21, 2012	53	2	55
2nd replacement	April 11, 2012	44	0	44

Round 3 Mailing	Date	U.S.	International	Total
Postcards	March 21, 2012	97	2	99
1st replacement	April 5, 2012	31	1	32
2nd replacement	April 25, 2012	20	0	20

Data analysis

Returned questionnaires were coded and the responses were processed using custom and standard statistical software applications—Statistical Analysis Software® (SAS), and a custom designed FileMaker Pro® application. Descriptive statistics and cross-tabulations were calculated for the coded data; responses to open-ended questions were categorized and summarized. Double-key data entry validation was performed on numeric and text entry variables and the remaining checkbox (bubble) variables were read by optical mark recognition (OMR) software.

Limitations

As with all surveys, this study has limitations that should be considered when interpreting the results.

1. This was a self-administered survey. Respondents completed the questionnaire after the visit, which may have resulted in poor recall. Thus, it is not possible to know whether visitor responses reflected actual behavior.

2. The data reflect visitor use patterns at the selected sites during the study period of January 27 – March 7, 2012. The results present a 'snapshot in time' and do not necessarily apply to visitors during other times of the year.

3. Caution is advised when interpreting any data with a sample size of less than 30, as the results may be unreliable. Whenever the sample size is less than 30, the word **"CAUTION!"** is included in the graph, figure, table, or text.

4. Occasionally, there may be inconsistencies in the results. Inconsistencies arise from missing data or incorrect answers (due to misunderstood directions, carelessness, or poor recall of information). Therefore, refer to both the percentage and N (number of individuals or visitor groups) when interpreting the results.

Special conditions

The weather during the survey period varied between sunny and warm to cool with occasional cloud cover and rain. Temperatures ranged from low 30s in the morning to 60 to 80 F in the afternoon. No special events occurred in the area that would have affected the type and amount of visitation to the park.

Checking nonresponse bias

Five variables were used to check non-response bias: participant age, group size, group type, how visit to the park fit in to travel plans, and participant proximity from home to the park. Respondents and nonrespondents were not statistically different in terms of group size and primary reason for visiting the area, but were significantly different in average age, group type, and proximity from home to the park (see Tables 3 - 6). The results indicated that there are potential nonresponse biases in the survey results. Respondents at younger age ranges (especially 40 and younger) may be underrepresented in the results. Visitors who traveled with friends, and visitors who lived within 51 to 100 miles radius of the park may also be underrepresented. See Appendix 3 for more details of the non-response bias checking procedures.

Table 3. Comparison of respondents and nonrespondents by average age and group size

Variable	Respondents	Nonrespondents	p-value (t-test)
Age (years)	52.36 (N=342)	41.98 (N=103)	<0.001
Group size	2.41 (N=333)	3.74 (N=100)	0.148

Table 4. Comparison of respondents and nonrespondents by group type

Group type	Respondents	Nonrespondents	p-value (chi-square)
Alone	61 (18%)	15 (15%)	
Family	193 (58%)	41 (41%)	
Friends	54 (16%)	38 (38%)	
Family and friends	24 (7%)	7 (7%)	
Other	2 (1%)	0 (0%)	
			0.008

Table 5. Comparison of respondents and nonrespondents by how park fit into travel plans

Destination	Respondents	Nonrespondents	p-value (chi-square)
Park as primary destination	246 (73%)	83 (19%)	
Park as one of several destinations	75 (22%)	17 (4%)	
Unplanned visit	15 (4%)	4 (1%)	
			0.389

Table 6. Comparison of respondents and nonrespondents by distance from home to park

Distance	Respondents	Nonrespondents	p-value (chi-square)
Within 50 miles	121 (37%)	54 (13%)	
51-100 miles	37 (11%)	14 (3%)	
100-200 miles	51 (16%)	14 (3%)	
201 miles or more	116 (35%)	20 (5%)	
International visitors	3 (1%)	2 (<1%)	
			0.016

Results

Group and Visitor Characteristics

Visitor group size

Question 19b
On this visit, how many people were in your personal group, including yourself?

Results
- 55% of visitor groups consisted of two people (see Figure 1).

- 18% were alone.

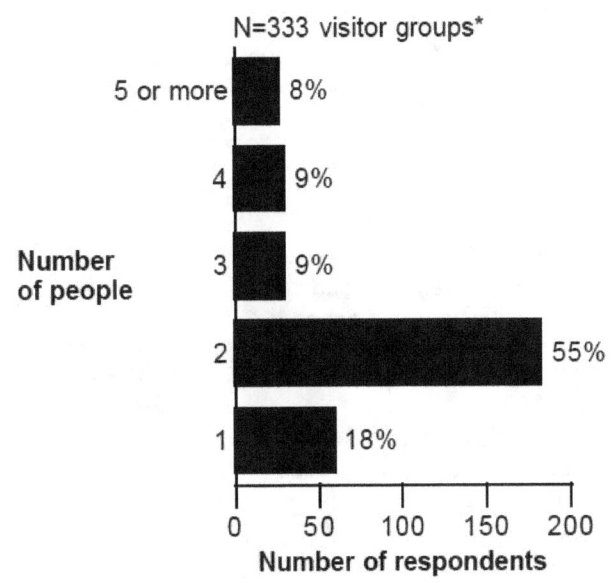

Figure 1. Visitor group size

Visitor group type

Question 19a
On this visit, what kind of personal group (not guided tour/school/other organized group) were you with?

Results
- 58% of visitor groups consisted of family members (see Figure 2).

- "Other" group type (1%) was:

    Co-workers

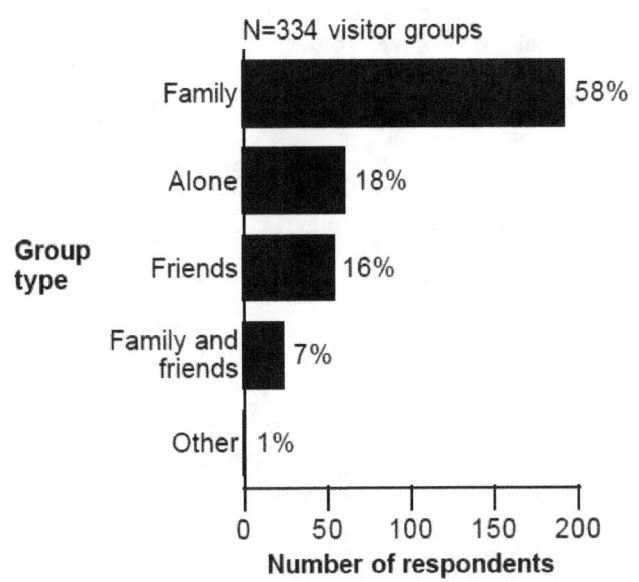

Figure 2. Visitor group type

Visitors with organized groups

Question 18a

On this visit, were you and your personal group with a commercial guided tour group?

Results

- No visitor groups were with a commercial guided tour group (see Figure 3).

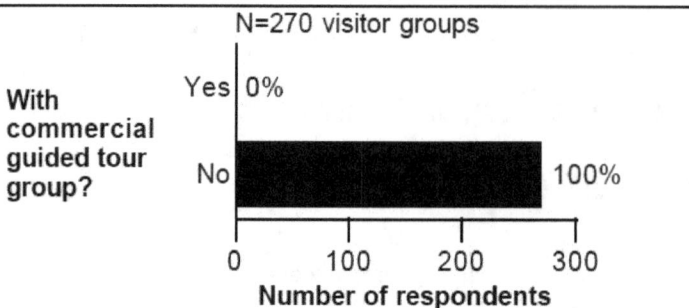

Figure 3. Visitors with a commercial guided tour group

Question 18b

On this visit, were you and your personal group with a school/educational group?

Results

- 4% of visitor groups were with a school/educational group (see Figure 4).

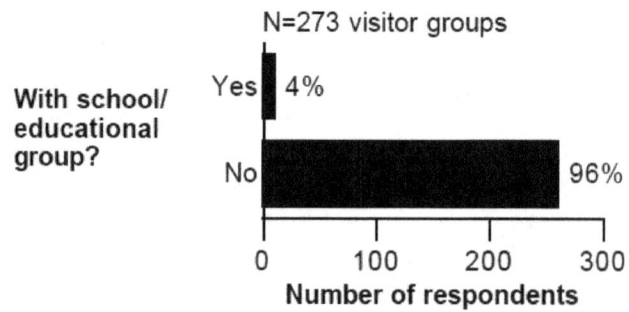

Figure 4. Visitors with a school/educational group

Question 18c

On this visit, were you and your personal group with an "other" organized group (scouts, work, church, etc.)?

Results

- 5% of visitor groups were with an "other" organized group (see Figure 5).

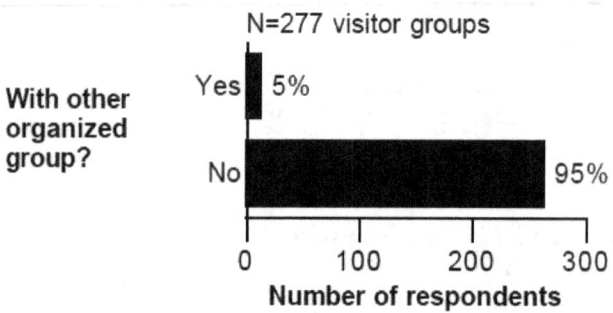

Figure 5. Visitors with an "other" organized group

Question 18d

If you were with one of these organized groups, how many people, including yourself, were in this group?

Results – Interpret with **CAUTION!**

- Not enough visitor groups responded to this question to provide reliable results (see Figure 6).

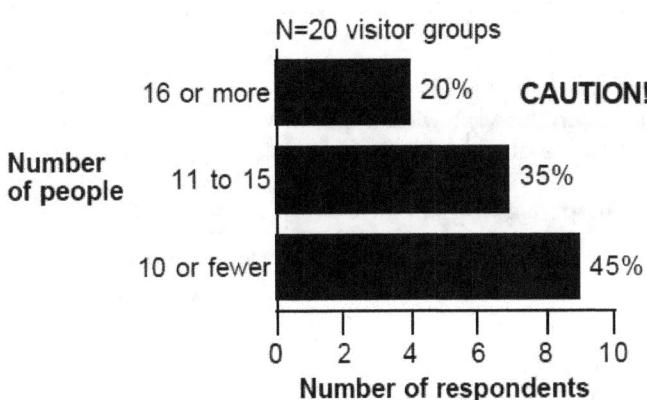

Figure 6. Organized group size

United States visitors by state of residence

Question 20b

For you and your personal group on this visit, what is your state of residence?

Note: Response was limited to 7 members from each visitor group.

Results

- U.S. visitors were from 34 states and comprised 98% of total visitation to the park during the survey period.

- 52% of U.S. visitors came from South Carolina (see Table 6 and Figure 7).

- 11% came from North Carolina.

- Smaller proportions came from 32 other states.

Table 6. United States visitors by state of residence

State	Number of visitors	Percent of U.S. visitors N=727 Individuals	Percent of total visitors N=743 Individuals
South Carolina	376	52%	51%
North Carolina	79	11%	11%
Ohio	27	4%	4%
New York	20	3%	3%
Georgia	19	3%	3%
Connecticut	18	2%	2%
Pennsylvania	18	2%	2%
Virginia	17	2%	2%
Massachusetts	16	2%	2%
Michigan	16	2%	2%
Florida	13	2%	2%
Indiana	11	2%	1%
22 other states	97	13%	13%

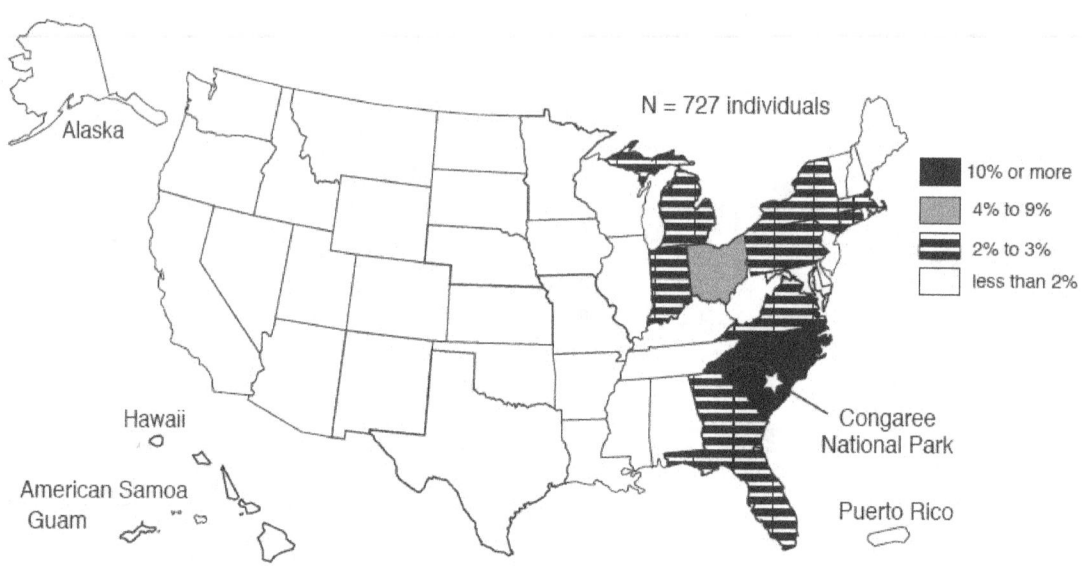

Figure 7. United States visitors by state of residence

Visitors from South Carolina and adjacent states by county of residence

Note: Response was limited to 7 members from each visitor group.

Results

- Visitors from South Carolina and adjacent states were from 65 counties and comprised 66% of the total U.S. visitation to the park during the survey period.

- 34% came from Richland County, SC (see Table 7).

- 18% came from Lexington County, SC.

- Smaller proportions of visitors came from 63 other counties in South Carolina and adjacent states.

Table 7. Visitors from South Carolina and adjacent states by county of residence

County, State	Number of visitors N=483 individuals	Percent*
Richland, SC	165	34
Lexington, SC	85	18
Mecklenburg, NC	20	4
Aiken, SC	17	4
Kershaw, SC	14	3
Beaufort, SC	13	3
Sumter, SC	11	2
Buncombe, NC	9	2
Greenville, SC	9	2
56 other counties	140	29

International visitors by country of residence

Question 20b

For you and your personal group on this visit, what is your country of residence?

Note: Response was limited to 7 members from each visitor group.

Results – **CAUTION!**

Not enough visitors responded to this question to provide reliable results (see Table 8).

Table 8. International visitors by country of residence

Country	Number of visitors	Percent of international visitors N=16 Individuals*	Percent of total visitors N=743 Individuals
Germany	5	31%	1%
Italy	3	19%	<1%
Canada	2	13%	<1%
France	2	13%	<1%
Israel	2	13%	<1%
Finland	1	6%	<1%
United Kingdom	1	6%	<1%

Number of visits to Congaree NP in past 12 months

Question 20c
For you and your personal group on this visit, how many times have you visited Congaree NP in the past 12 months (including this visit)?

Note: Response was limited to 7 members from each visitor group.

Results
- 78% of visitors visited the park once in the past 12 months (see Figure 8).

- 10% of visitors visited two times.

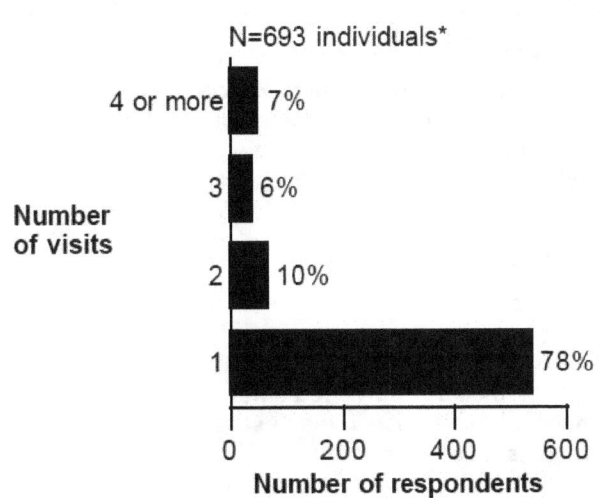

Figure 8. Number of visits to park in past 12 months

Number of lifetime visits to Congaree NP

Question 20d
For you and your personal group on this visit, how many times have you visited Congaree NP in your lifetime (including this visit)?

Note: Response was limited to 7 members from each visitor group.

Results
- 63% of visitors visited the park once in their lifetime (see Figure 9).

- 19% of visitors visited four or more times.

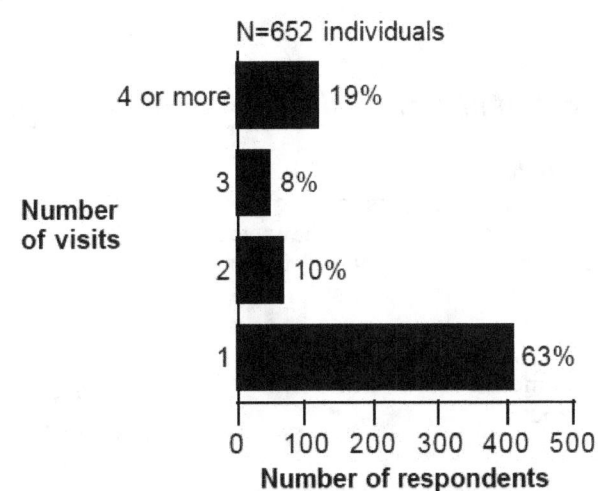

Figure 9. Number of visits to park in lifetime

Number of visits to other national parks in past 12 months

Question 20e

For you and your personal group on this visit, how many times have you visited other national parks in the past 12 months (including this visit)?

Note: Response was limited to 7 members from each visitor group.

Results

- 27% of visitors had visited other national parks once in the past 12 months (see Figure 10).

- 26% had visited other national parks five or more times.

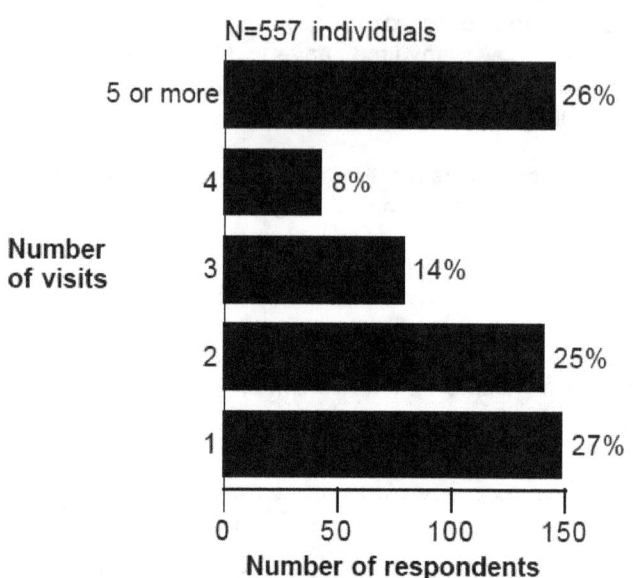

Figure 10. Number of visits to other national parks in past 12 months

Number of lifetime visits to other national parks

Question 20f

For you and your personal group on this visit, how many times have you visited other national parks in your lifetime (including this visit)?

Note: Response was limited to 7 members from each visitor group.

Results

33% of visitors had visited other national parks 21 or more times in their lifetime (see Figure 11).

- 24% had visited other national parks between one and five times.

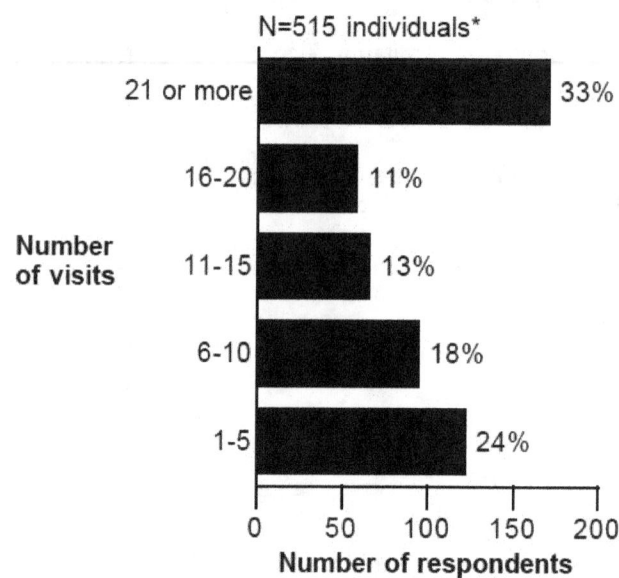

Figure 11. Number of visits to other national parks in lifetime

Visitor age

Question 20a

For you and your personal group on this visit, what is your current age?

Note: Response was limited to seven members from each visitor group.

Results

- Visitor ages ranged from one to 88 years.

- 47% were 51-70 years old (see Figure 12).

- 22% were 31-50 years old.

- 12% of visitors were 15 years or younger

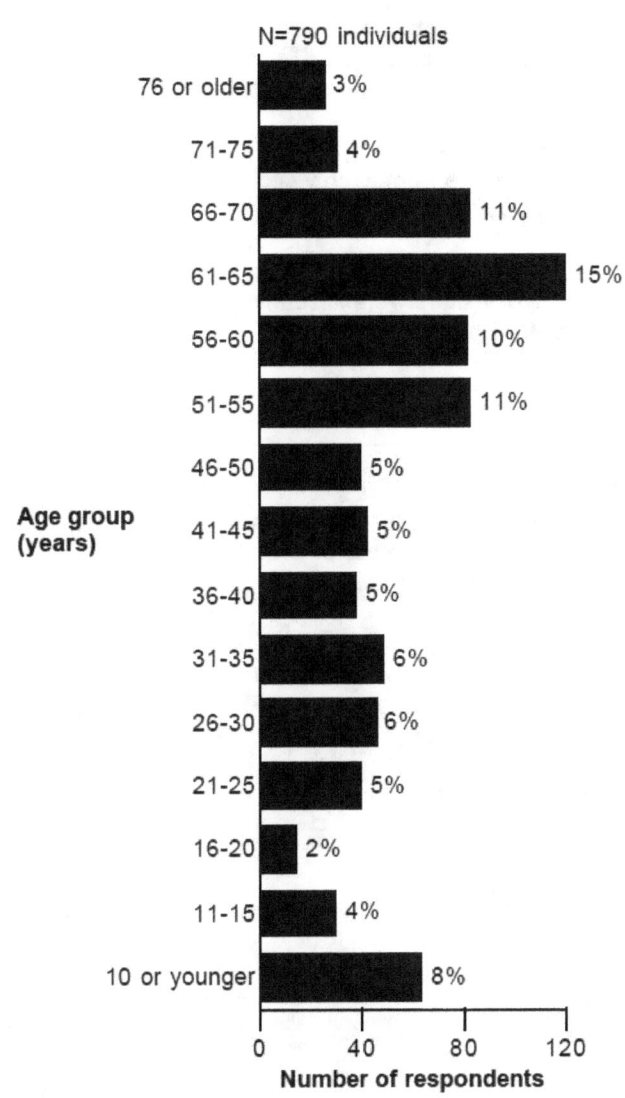

Figure 12. Visitor age

Visitor ethnicity

Question 23a

Are you or members of your personal group Hispanic or Latino?

Note: Response was limited to 7 members from each visitor group.

Results

- 1% of visitors were Hispanic or Latino (see Figure 13).

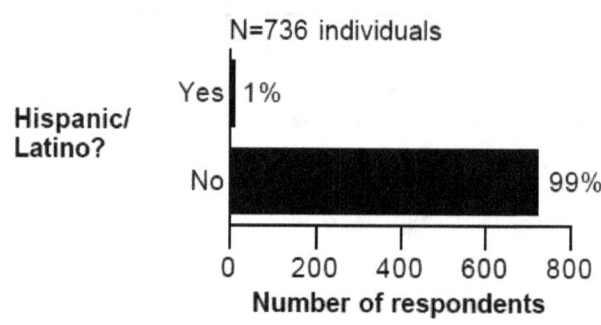

Figure 13. Visitors who were Hispanic or Latino

Visitor race

Question 23b

What is your race? What is the race of each member of your personal group?

Note: Response was limited to 7 members from each visitor group.

Results

- 94% of visitors were White (see Figure 14).

- 3% were Asian.

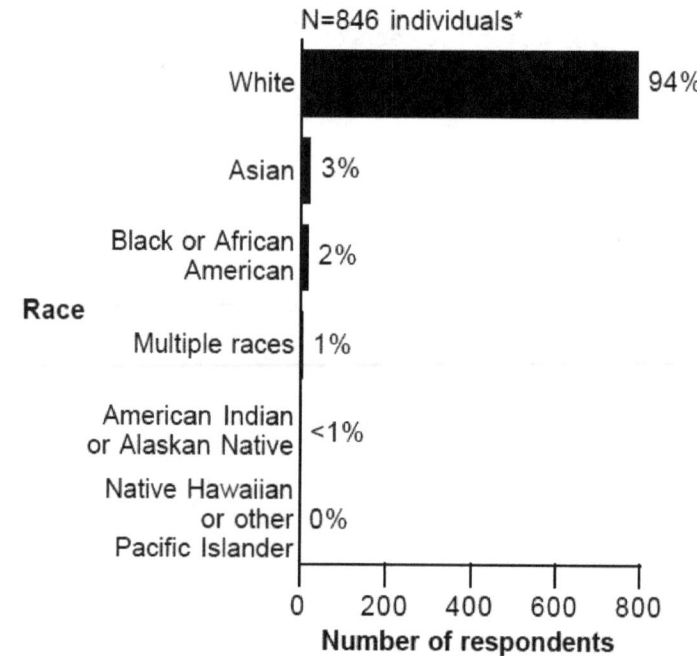

Figure 14. Visitor race

Visitors with physical conditions affecting access/participation

Question 22a

Does anyone in your personal group have mobility or other physical impairments?

Results
- 6% of visitor groups included individuals with mobility or other physical conditions (see Figure 15).

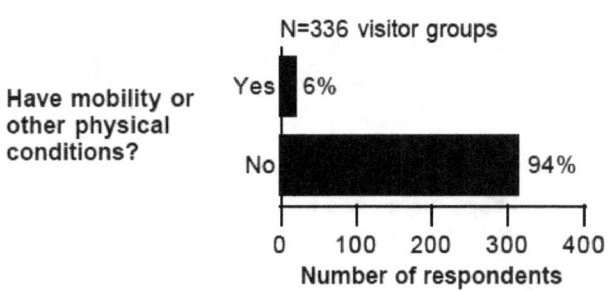

N=336 visitor groups

Have mobility or other physical conditions?

Yes 6%

No 94%

Number of respondents

Figure 15. Visitor groups that had members with mobility or other physical conditions

Question 22b

If YES, did anyone in your personal group have a physical condition that made it difficult to access or participate in park activities or services?

Results – Interpret with **CAUTION!**
- Not enough visitor groups responded to provide reliable results (see Figure 16).

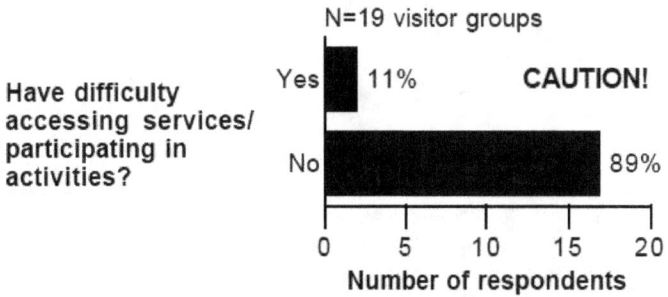

N=19 visitor groups

Have difficulty accessing services/ participating in activities?

Yes 11%   **CAUTION!**

No 89%

Number of respondents

Figure 16. Visitor groups that had members with physical conditions affecting access to services or participation in park activities

Respondent level of education

Question 21
For you only, what is the highest level of education you have completed?

Results
- 39% of respondents had a graduate degree (see Figure 17).

- 38% of respondents had a bachelor's degree.

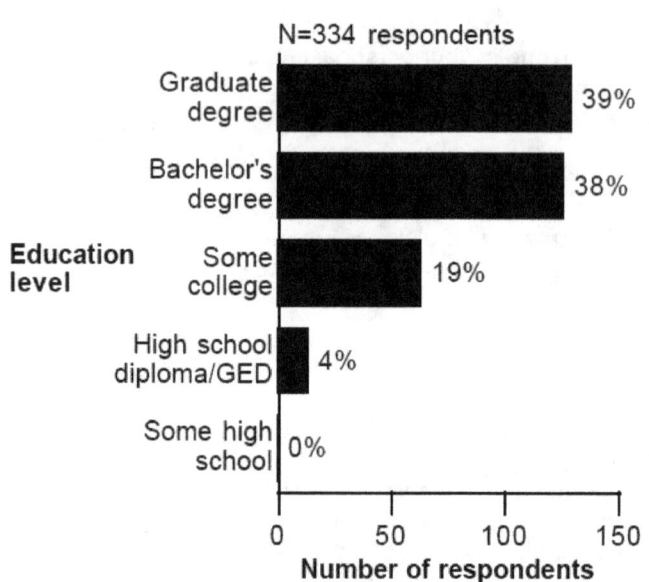

Figure 17. Respondent level of education

Respondent household income

Question 25a

Which category best represents your annual household income?

Results

- 53% of respondents had an income between $50,000 and $149,999 (see Figure 18).

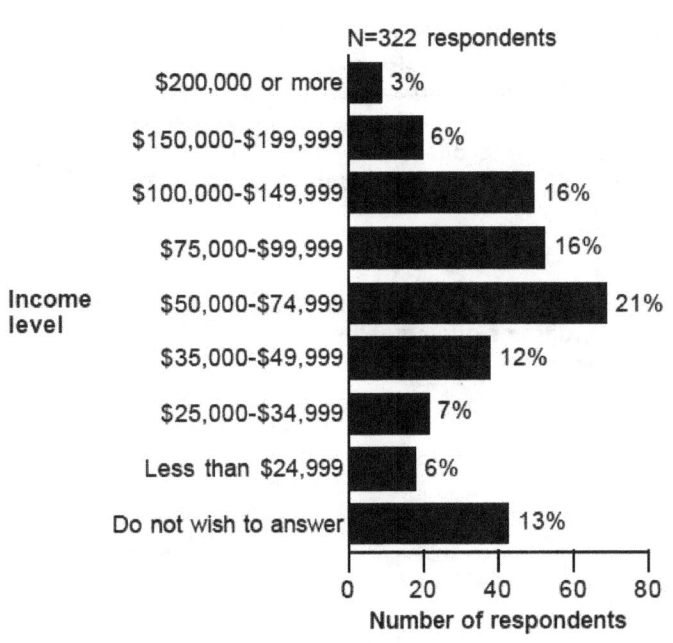

Figure 18. Respondent household level of income

Respondent household size

Question 25b

How many people are in your household?

Results

- 54% of respondents had two people in their household (see Figure 19).

- 19% of households consisted of one person.

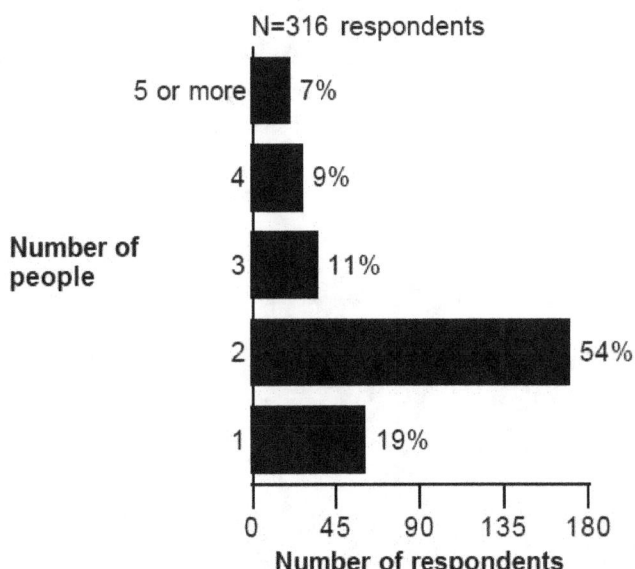

Figure 19. Number of people in household

Awareness of park programs

Question 2

Prior to your visit, were you and your personal group aware of programs (ranger-led walks, canoe trips, presentations, school group tours, etc.) offered in Congaree NP?

Results

- 65% of visitor groups were aware of programs offered at the park (see Figure 20).

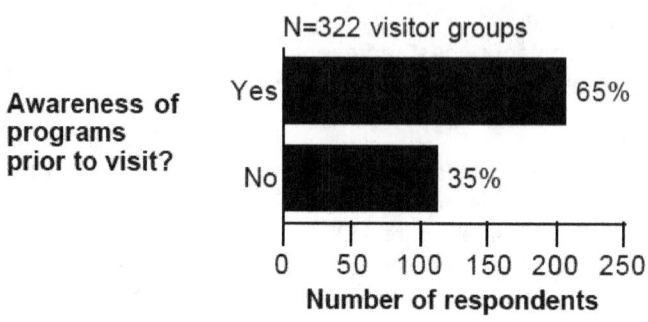

Figure 20. Visitor groups that were aware of programs in Congaree NP

Park name change and decision to visit

Question 3a

In 2003, Congaree Swamp National Monument became Congaree NP. Did this name change have any effect on your decision to visit?

Results

- 19% of respondents said their decision to visit was affected by the name change (see Figure 21).

Question 3b

If YES, what effect did it have? (Open-ended)

Results

- 66 respondents commented on the effect of the park's name change (see Table 9.)

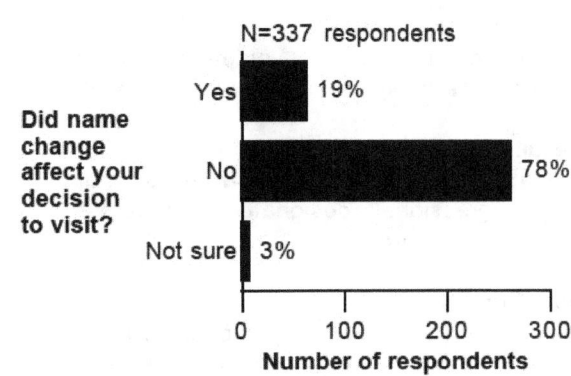

Figure 21. Respondents for whom the name change affected decision to visit

Table 9. Effect of name change on decision to visit
(N=66 comments; some visitor groups made more than one comment.)

Comment	Number of times mentioned
Visiting all national parks	24
More interested in visiting a national park	10
Increased pride/prestige	5
National park more appealing	5
Word swamp is not appealing	4
National park designation seems more important	3
Only visit national parks	2
Standards/services of a national park	2
Always wanted to visit a national park	1
Appears on a national park map	1
Learned of the park because of the name change	1
Like to visit national parks	1
Listed in guides to national parks	1
National park seems wilder and more unique	1
National park sounds better	1
Our 48th national park	1
Special to be a national park	1
Wanted to see a national park in our state	1
Wanted to visit a new national park	1

Knowledge of congressionally designated wilderness

Question 4a

Prior to your visit, were you aware of what congressionally designated wilderness is?

Results

- 59% of respondents were aware of what congressionally designated wilderness is (see Figure 22).

Question 4b

If NO, did you and your personal group learn about congressionally designated wilderness during your visit?

Results

- 43% of visitor groups said they learned about congressionally designated wilderness at Congaree NP during their visit (see Figure 23).

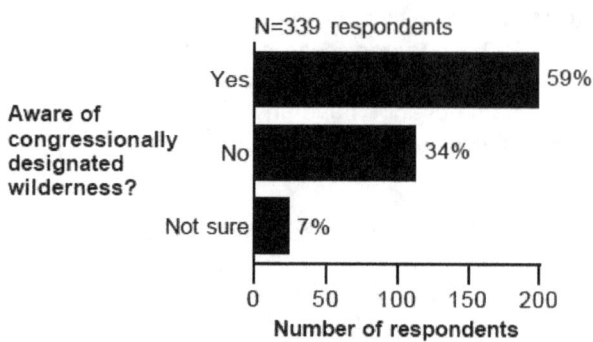

Figure 22. Respondents who were aware of what congressionally designated wilderness is

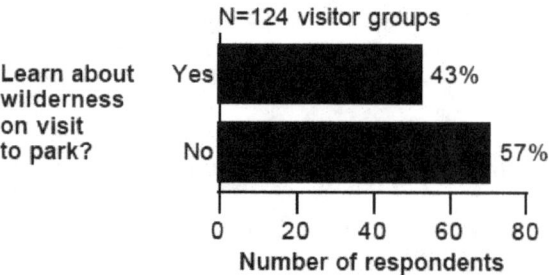

Figure 23. Visitor groups that learned about congressionally designated wilderness at park

Park policy to remove non-native species

Question 5

The National Park Service has a policy to control or remove non-native plants and animals from within park boundaries. Non-native species occupy an area that is not part of their natural, historic range, and often originated from another continent or region. Many of these species are invasive and damage park resources. Were you aware of this policy prior to your visit to Congaree NP?

Results

- 50% of respondents were aware of the policy to remove non-native species (see Figure 24).

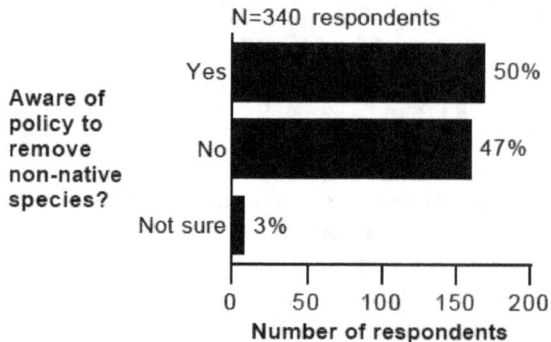

Figure 24. Respondents aware of park policy regarding non-native species

Support for policy to remove non-native species

Question 6
Would you and your personal group be supportive of the control and removal of non-native species at Congaree NP?

Results
- 86% of visitor groups were supportive of the removal of non-native plants (see Figure 25).

- 77% were supportive of the removal of non-native animals (see Figure 26).

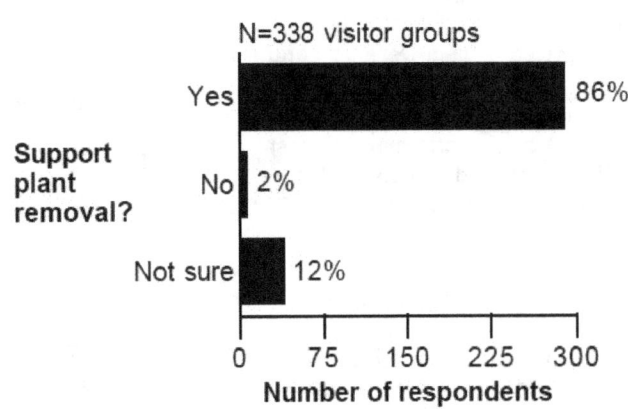

Figure 25. Visitor groups supporting the removal of non-native plants

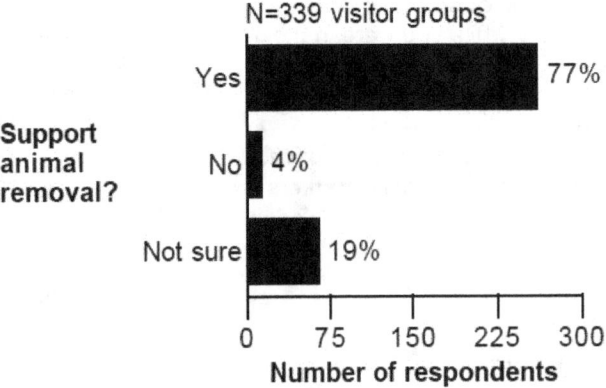

Figure 26. Visitor groups supporting the removal of non-native animals

Awareness of research and education in the park

Question 15a

Prior to this visit, were you and your personal group aware that Congaree NP is the home to the Old-Growth Bottomland Forest Research and Education Center, one of 21 centers nationwide?

Results

- 24% of visitor groups were aware of the Old-Growth Bottomland Forest Research and Education Center before their visit (see Figure 27).

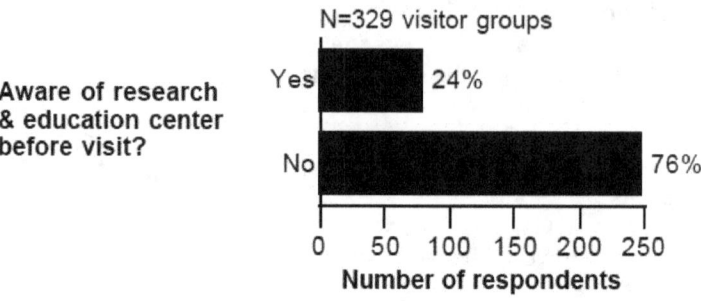

Figure 27. Visitor groups that were aware of the Old-Growth Bottomland Forest Research and Education Center before visit

Question 15b

Did you and your personal group notice any scientists, scientific markers, or scientific equipment at work while you were in the park?

Results

- 47% of visitor groups noticed scientists, scientific markers, or scientific equipment at work in the park (see Figure 28).

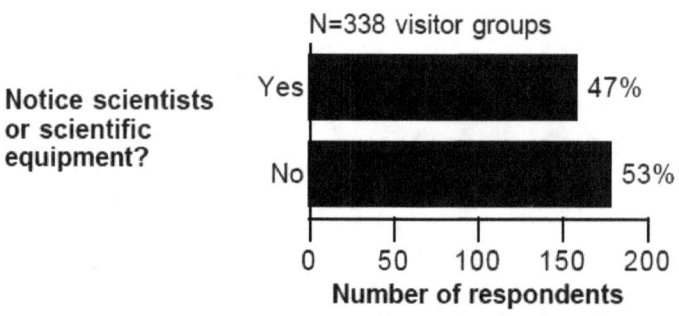

Figure 28. Visitor groups that noticed scientists, scientific markers, or scientific equipment at work during this visit

Question 15c

Did you and your personal group – through programs and products – learn about actual results of scientific studies at the park?

Results

- 26% of visitor groups learned about scientific results through programs and products while in the park (see Figure 29).

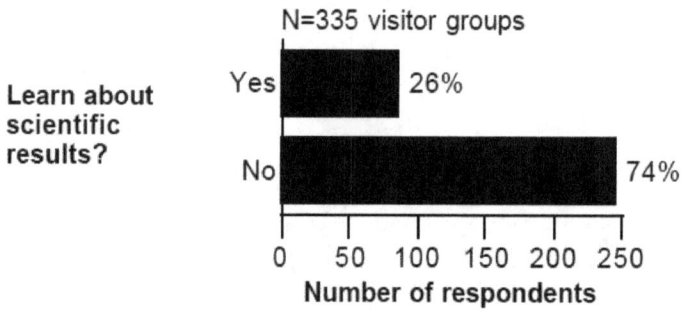

Figure 29. Visitor groups that learned about current scientific results in the park

Trip/Visit Characteristics and Preferences

Information sources prior to visit

Question 1

Prior to your visit, how did you and your personal group obtain information about Congaree NP?

Results

- 94% of visitor groups obtained information about Congaree NP prior to their visit (see Figure 30).

- As shown in Figure 31, among those visitor groups that obtained information about Congaree NP prior to their visit, the most common sources were:

  56% Park website
  30% Friends/relatives/word of mouth
  29% Previous visits

- 9% of visitor groups used other websites to obtain information prior to visit (see Table 10).

- Other sources of information used prior to visit (5%) are shown in Table 11.

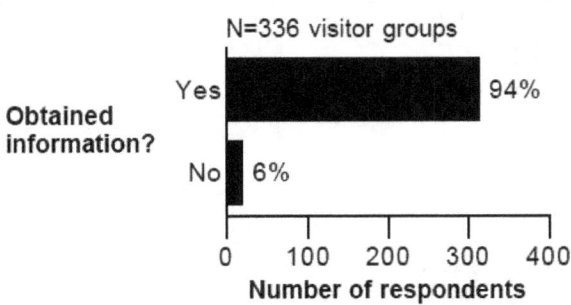

Figure 30. Visitor groups that obtained information prior to visit

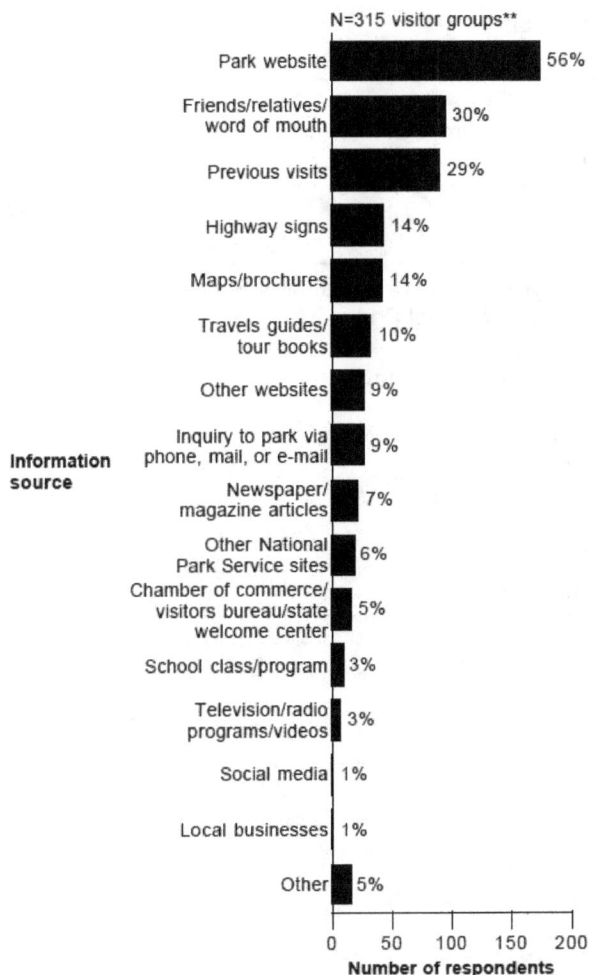

Figure 31. Sources of information

Table 10. "Other" websites used to obtain information prior to visit
(N= 26 comments)

Element	Number of times mentioned
Google	9
SC State Parks	2
tripadvisor.com	2
Birding websites	1
birdsource.org	1
congareeriver.org	1
Friends of Congaree National Park website	1
Mapquest	1
SC Information Highway	1
scgreatoutdoors.com	1
sctrails.net	1
volunteer.gov	1
waterdata.usgs.gov	1
Wikipedia	1
wildlifesouth.com	1
Yahoo	1

Table 11. "Other" sources of information used prior to visit
(N= 13 comments)

Element	Number of times mentioned
National Geographic Guide to National Parks of US	2
Passport to your National Parks	2
50 Hikes in South Carolina	1
Artwork of nephew on display	1
Church	1
Congaree Pottery	1
Friends of Congaree Swamp	1
Ken Burns' National Parks	1
National Park Book	1
National Parks Companion app	1
National parks iPhone app	1

Park as destination

Question from on-site interview

A two-minute interview was conducted with each individual selected to complete the questionnaire. During the interview, the question was asked: "How did this visit to Congaree NP fit into your personal group's travel plans?"

Results

- 75% of visitor groups indicated that the park was their primary destination (see Figure 32).

- 21% said the park was one of several destinations.

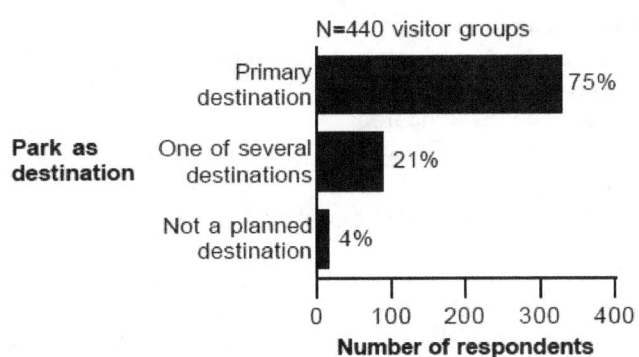

Figure 32. How visit to park fit into visitor groups' travel plans

Alternate recreation site

Question 24a

On this trip, if you and your personal group had not chosen to visit Congaree NP, what other recreation site would you have visited instead? (Open-ended)

Results

- 58% of visitor groups (N=197) responded to this question.

- Table 12 lists the places that visitor groups indicated as potential alternate sites they would have visited instead of Congaree NP.

Table 12. Alternate recreation sites
(N=220 comments; some visitor groups listed more than one site)

Site	Number of times mentioned
None	45
Harbison State Park/Forest	13
Unsure	10
Riverbanks Zoo	8
Lake Murray	7
Peachtree Rock Preserve	7
South Carolina State Museum	7
State park	7
Charleston, SC	6
Poinsett State Park	6
Sesquicentennial State Park	6
Zoo	6
Came specifically for Congaree	4
Museum	3
Places to hike	3
Smoky Mountains	3
Another state or national park	2
Cowpens	2
Crowders Mountain State Park	2
Florida	2
Fort Sumter	2
Pisgah National Forest	2
Riverwalk	2
Saluda River	2
Other locations	63

Question 24b

How far is this alternative site from your home?

Results

- 52% of the visitor groups indicated that they would travel up to 50 miles from their home to visit the alternate site (see Figure 33).

- 28% would travel 201 or more miles.

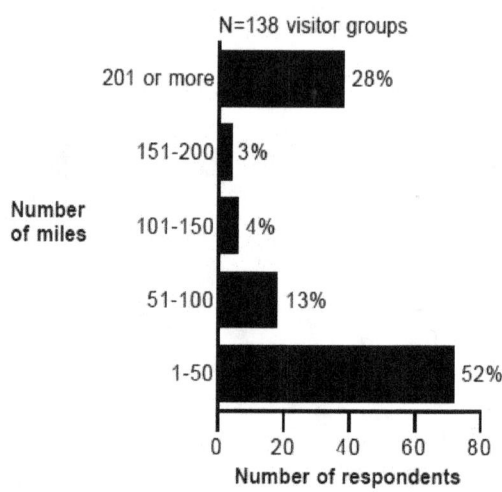

Figure 33. Number of miles to alternate recreation site

Primary reason for visiting the park area

Question 7

On this trip, what was the primary reason that you and your personal group came to the Congaree NP area (within 1-hour drive of the park)?

Results

- 28% of visitor groups were residents of the area (see Figure 34).

- As shown in Figure 35, the most common primary reasons for visiting the area (within a 1-hour drive of the park) among nonresident visitor groups were:

      65% Visit the park
      12% Visit friends/relatives in
          the area

- Other primary reasons (8%) were:

      Camping
      Conference
      Enjoy nature with family/friends
      Exercise
      Family fun
      Hiking
      Mountain biking
      Overnight canoe trip
      Photography
      School
      See nephew's artwork
      Stress release
      Travel through - planned visit

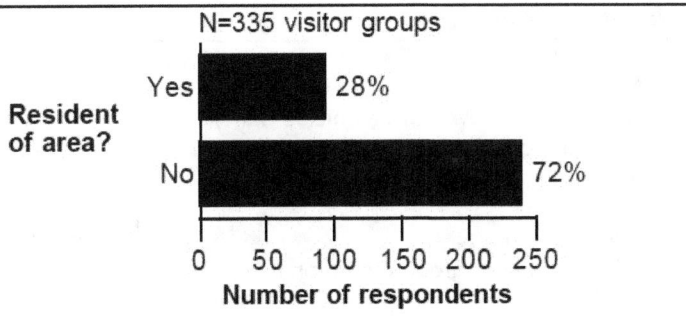

Figure 34. Residents of the area (within a 1-hour drive of the park)

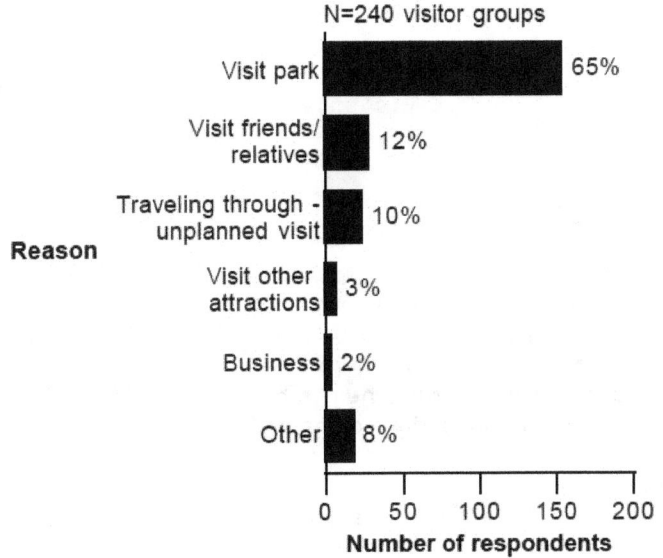

Figure 35. Primary reason for visiting the park area (within a 1-hour drive of the park)

Number of vehicles

Question 12

On this visit, how many vehicles did you and your personal group use to arrive at the park?

Results

- 92% of visitor groups used one vehicle to arrive at the park (see Figure 36).

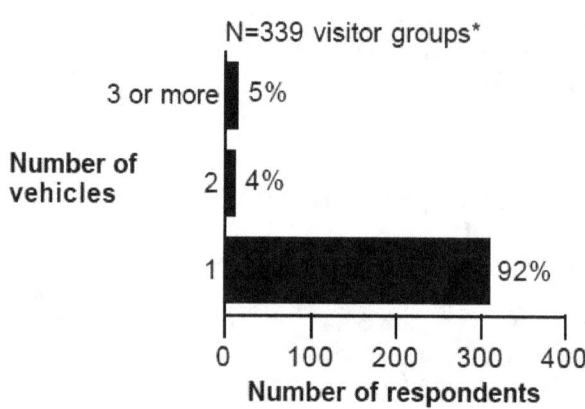

Figure 36. Number of vehicles used to arrive at the park

Overnight stays

Question 9a

On this trip, did you and your personal group stay overnight away from your permanent residence either inside Congaree NP or within the nearby area (within 1-hour drive of the park)?

Results

38% of visitor groups stayed overnight away from home either in the park or within a 1-hour drive of the park (see Figure 37).

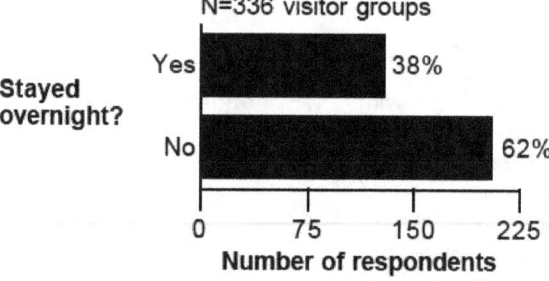

Figure 37. Visitor groups that stayed overnight in the park or within a 1-hour drive of the park

Question 9b

If YES, how many nights did you and your personal group spend inside the park?

Results

- 52% of visitor groups spent one night in the park (see Figure 38).

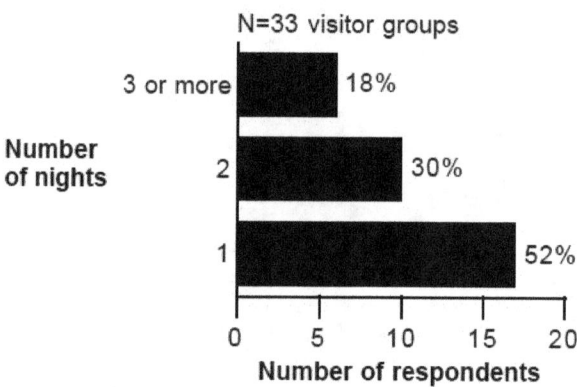

Figure 38. Number of nights spent inside the park

Question 9c

If YES, how many nights did you and your personal group spend outside the park within a 1-hour drive?

Results

- 49% of visitor groups stayed one night outside the park within a 1-hour drive of the park (see Figure 39).

- 35% stayed two or three nights.

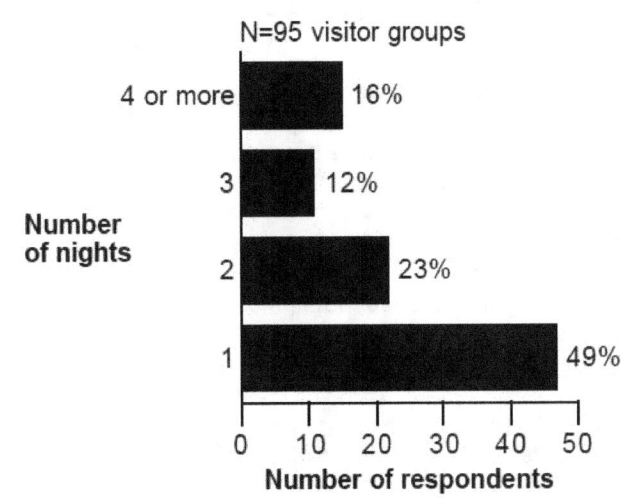

Figure 39. Number of nights spent in the area outside the park (within a 1-hour drive of the park).

Accommodations used inside the park

Question 9b

In which types of accommodations did you and your personal group spend the nights inside the park?

Results

- As shown in Figure 40, the most common types of accommodations used by visitor groups were:

      48% Tent camping
      27% Backcountry camping

- Table 13 shows the number of nights spent in accommodations inside the park.

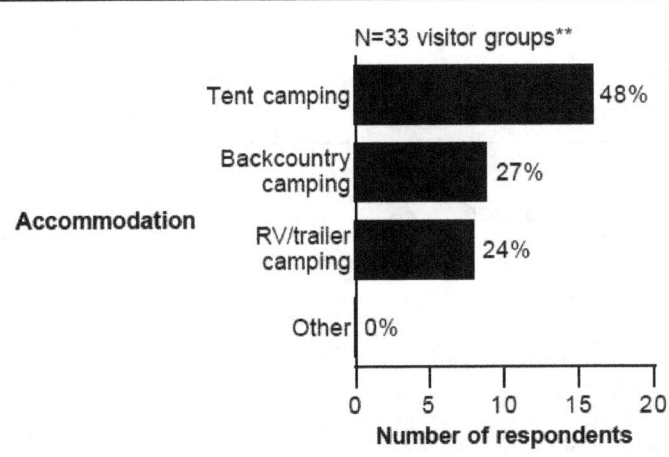

Figure 40. Accommodations used inside the park

Table 13. Number of nights spent in accommodations inside the park
(N=number of visitor groups)

Accommodation	N	Number of nights (%)*			
		1	2	3	4 or more
RV/trailer camping – **CAUTION!**	8	50	25	13	13
Tent camping - **CAUTION!**	16	31	44	25	0
Backcountry camping - **CAUTION!**	9	89	11	0	0
Other	0	–	–	–	–

Accommodations used outside the park

Question 9c

In which types of accommodations did you and your personal group spend the nights outside park within a 1-hour drive?

Results

- 82% of visitor groups stayed overnight in a lodge, hotel, motel, cabin, rented condo/home, or bed & breakfast (see Figure 41).

- Table 14 shows the number of nights spent in accommodations outside the park within a 1-hour drive of the park.

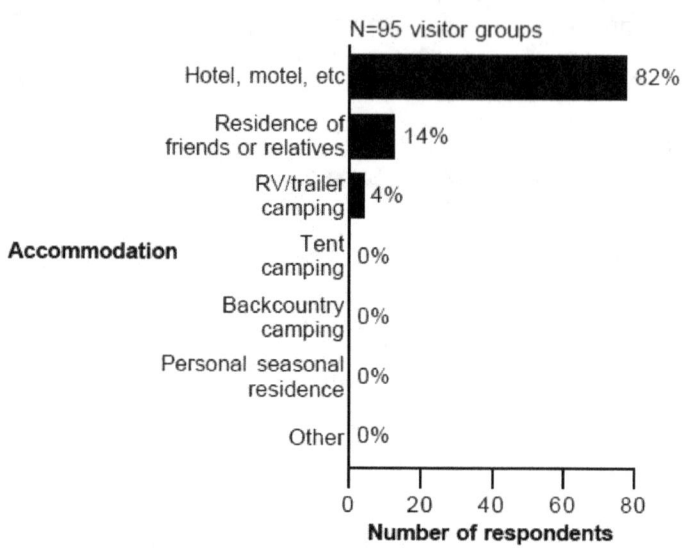

Figure 41. Accommodations used outside the park within a 1-hour drive

Table 14. Number of nights spent in accommodations outside the park within a 1-hour drive (N=number of visitor groups that specified the number of nights spent in each type of accommodation)

Accommodation	N	Number of nights (%) *			
		1	2	3	4 or more
Lodge, hotel, motel, cabin, rented condo/home, or bed & breakfast	78	51	23	13	13
RV/trailer camping – **CAUTION!**	4	50	50	–	–
Tent camping	0	–	–	–	–
Backcountry camping	0	–	–	–	–
Personal seasonal residence	0	–	–	–	–
Residence of friends or relatives – **CAUTION!**	13	38	15	8	38
Other	0	–	–	–	–

Note: Some visitor groups indicated they used an accommodation without specifying the number of nights; therefore, the N in Figure 41 and in Table 12 is different.

Length of stay in the park

Question 13b

On this visit, how long did you and your personal group spend visiting Congaree NP?

Results

<u>Number of hours if less than 24</u>

- 50% spent 3-4 hours in the park (see Figure 42).

- 24% of visitor groups 1-2 hours.

- The average length of stay for visitor groups that spent less than 24 hours was 3.8 hours.

<u>Number of days if 24 hours or more</u>

- Interpret with **CAUTION!** Not enough visitor groups responded to provide reliable results (see Figure 43).

- The average length of stay for visitor groups that spent more than 24 hours was 2.3 days.

<u>Average length of stay for all visitors</u>

- The average length of stay in the park for all visitor groups was 8.8 hours or 0.4 days.

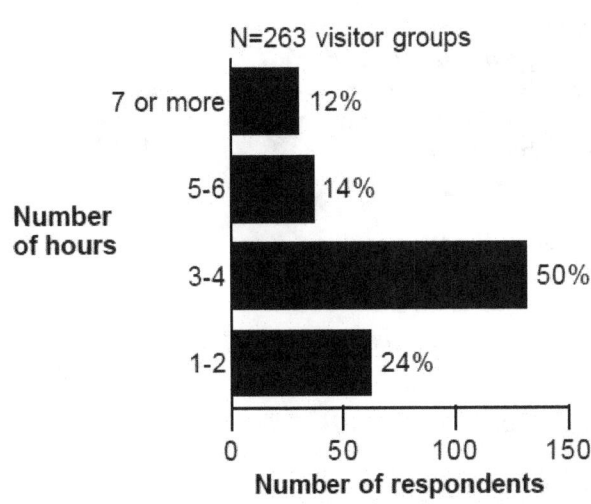

Figure 42. Number of hours spent in the park

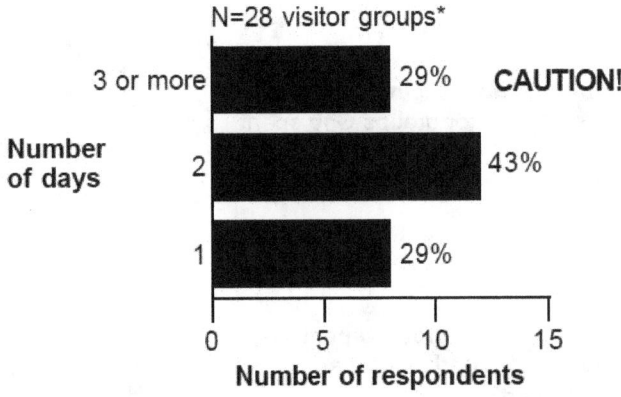

Figure 43. Number of days spent in the park

Length of stay in the park area

Question 13a

How long did you and your personal group stay in the Congaree NP area (within 1-hour drive of the park)?

Results

- 29% of visitor groups were residents of the area within a 1-hour drive of the park (see Figure 44).

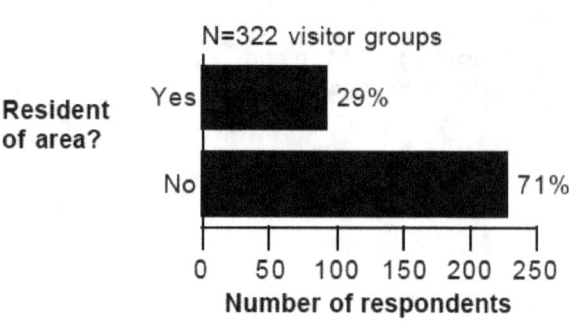

Figure 44. Residents of the area (within a 1-hour drive of the park)

Number of hours if less than 24

- 39% of visitor groups spent 3-4 hours in the park area (see Figure 45).

- 28% spent 1-2 hours.

- 17% spent 5-6 hours.

- The average length of stay in the area for visitor groups who spent less than 24 hours was 4.7 hours.

Number of days if 24 hours or more

- 60% of visitor groups spent 1-2 days in the park area (see Figure 46).

- 33% spent 3-4 days.

- The average length of stay for visitor groups that spent 24 hours or more was 3.4 days.

Average length of stay for all visitors

- The average length of stay for all visitor groups was 31.4 hours, or 1.3 days.

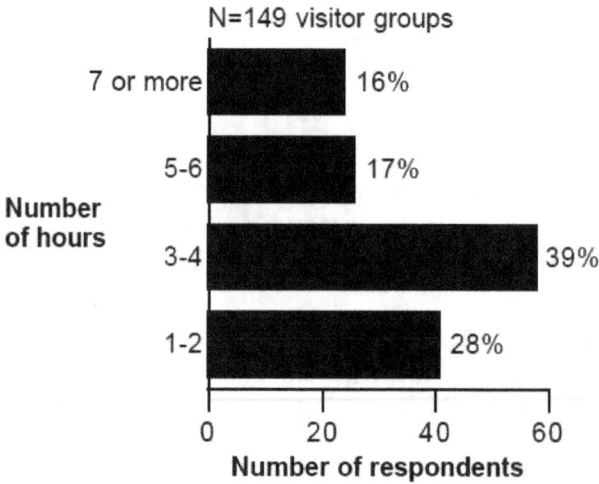

Figure 45. Number of hours spent in the park area (within a 1-hour drive of the park)

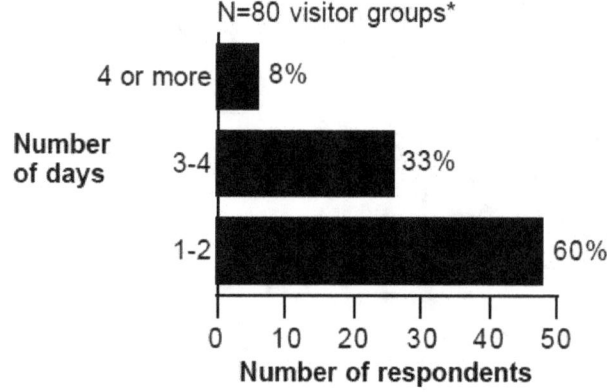

Figure 46. Number of days spent in the park area (within a 1-hour drive of the park)

Sites visited in the Congaree NP area

Question 8

On this visit, which sites did you and your personal group visit in the Congaree NP area (within 1-hour drive of the park)?

- As shown in Figure 47, the sites most commonly visited in the Congaree NP area were:

    26% The State Capitol
    23% Riverbanks Zoo
    21% University of South
        Carolina

- The least visited site was:

    1% National Advocacy Center

- "Other" sites (21%) visited are shown in Table 15.

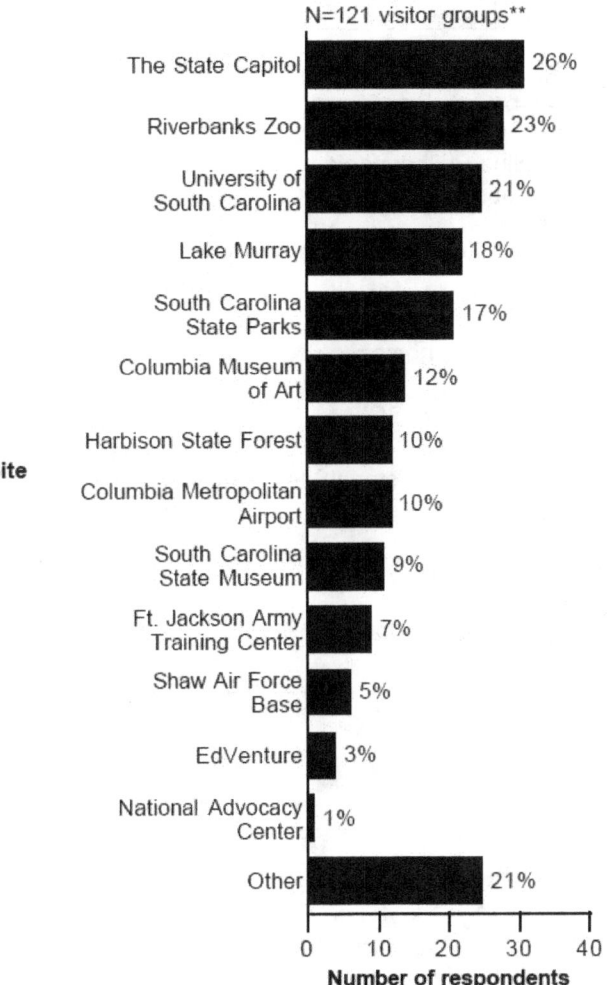

Figure 47. Sites visited in the park area (within a 1-hour drive of the park)

Table 15. "Other" sites visited in the park area
(N=21 comments)

Site	Number of times mentioned
Columbia, SC	3
South Carolina Philharmonic	2
Beidler Audubon Preserve	1
Boardwalk trail	1
Carolina Sandhills Wildlife	1
Cedar Creek	1
Charleston, SC	1
Downtown historic homes	1
Edisto Memorial Gardens	1
Geographic center of SC	1
Riverbanks Botanical Gardens	1
Rivers Bridge State Historic Site	1
Saint Matthews	1
Santee	1
Santee Wildlife Refuge	1
Shopping, job fairs	1
State fairgrounds garage sale	1
The Vista	1

Activities within the park

Question 11
On this visit, in which activities
did you and your personal
group participate within
Congaree NP?

Results
- As shown in Figure 48, the
  most common activities in
  which visitor groups
  participated were:

  85% Walking/hiking
  71% Visiting the visitor
       center
  25% Birdwatching
  14% Nature study (other
       than birdwatching)
  12% Picnicking

- "Other" activities (8%) were:

  Bible study
  Guided tour with John
    Cely
  Junior Ranger program
  Met with park ranger for
    school project
  Passport stamp
  Photography
  Reading maps charts
  Self-guided tour
  Watched film on park
  Watched video at visitor
    center

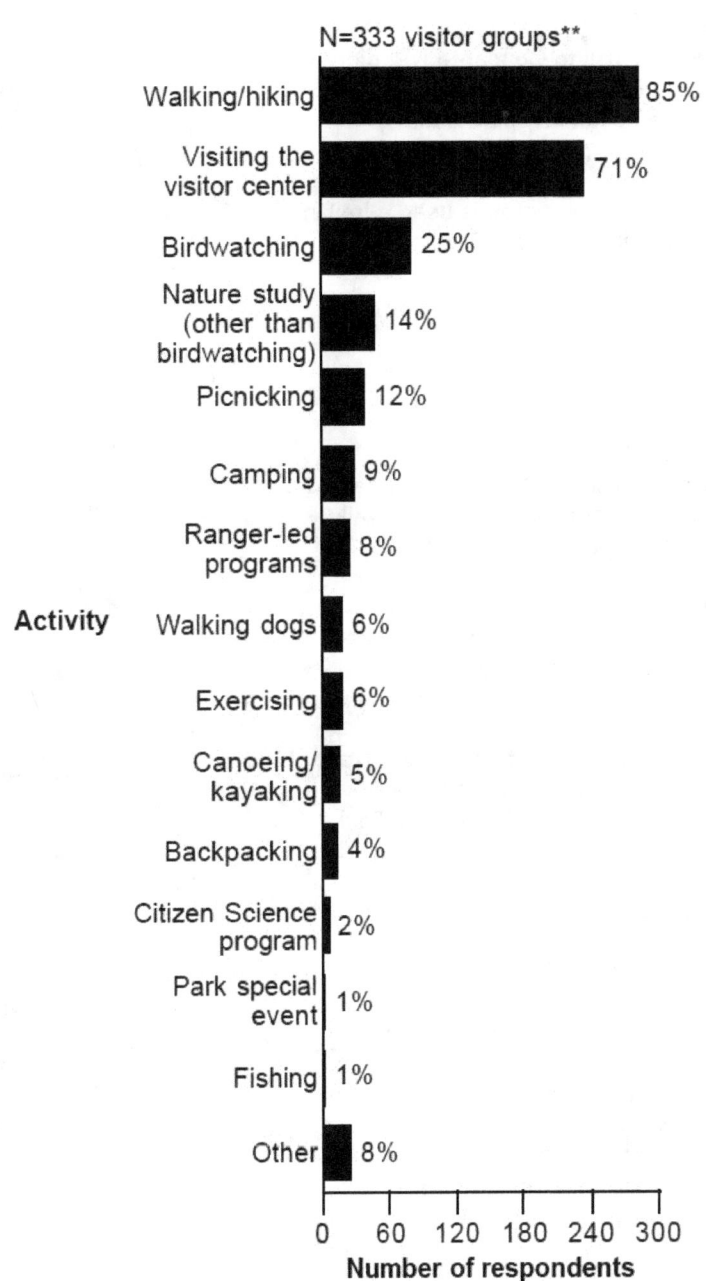

Figure 48. Activities on this visit

Use of park trails

Question 10a

On this visit to Congaree NP, did you and your personal group walk/canoe/kayak any park trails?

Results

- 96% of visitor groups used a trail in Congaree NP (see Figure 49).

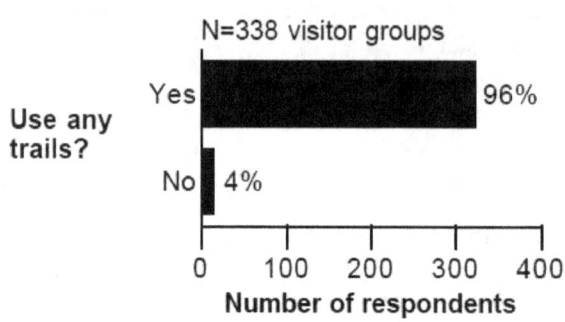

Figure 49. Visitor groups that used park trails

Question 10b

If YES, which of the following trails did you and your personal group walk/canoe/kayak on this visit?

Results

- As shown in Figure 50, of those visitor groups that used park trails, the most commonly used trails were:

  79% Elevated Boardwalk Trail
  70% Low Boardwalk Trail
  41% Weston Lake Loop Trail

- The least used trail was the Kingsnake Trail (5%).

- Other trails (2%) were:

  All trails around visitor center
  Big Tree guided walk
  Big Tree Hill
  Dog trail cutoff to visitor center
  Dogwalk trail
  Looped down to river

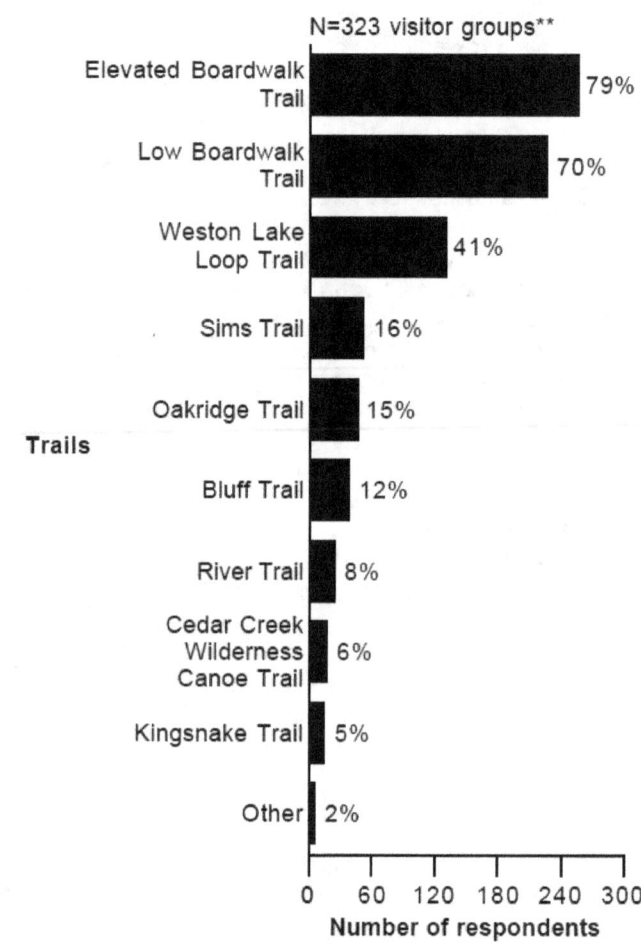

Figure 50. Trails used in Congaree NP

Ratings of Services, Facilities, Attributes, Resources, and Elements

Information services and facilities used

Question 16a
Please indicate all of the information services and facilities that you or your personal group used at Congaree NP during this visit.

Results
- As shown in Figure 51, the most common information services and facilities used by visitor groups were:

  90% Park brochure/map
  83% Assistance from park staff
  75% Visitor center exhibits

- The least used service/facility was ranger-guided canoe tours (2%).

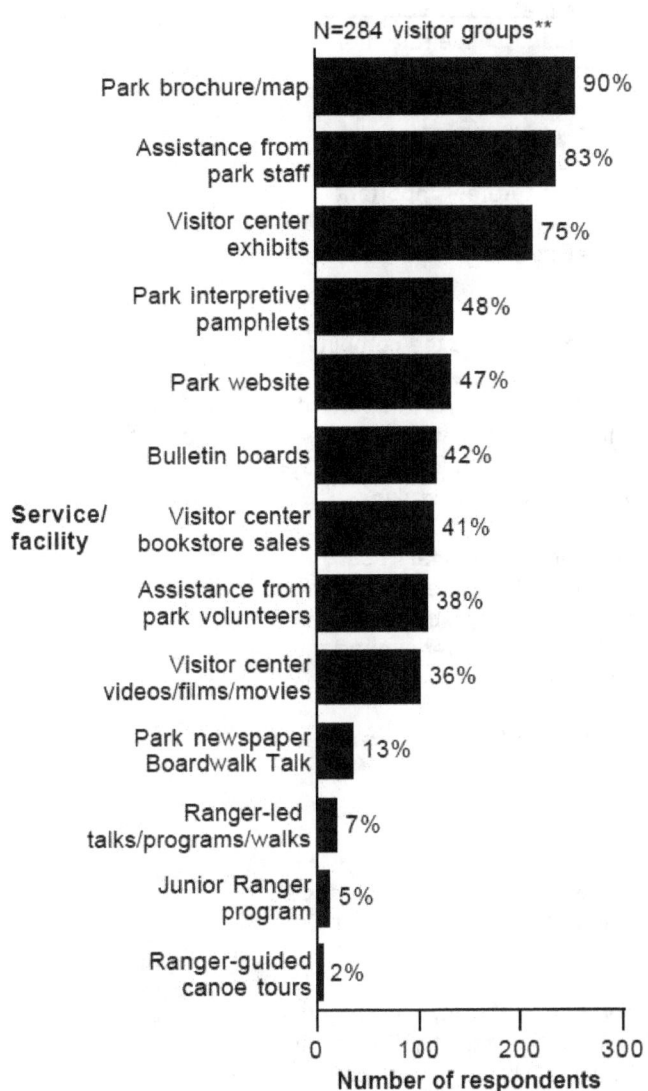

Figure 51. Information services and facilities used

Importance ratings of information services and facilities

Question 16b

For only those services and facilities that you or your personal group used, please rate their importance to your visit from 1-5.

1=Not important
2=Somewhat important
3=Moderately important
4=Very important
5=Extremely important

Results

- Figure 52 shows the combined proportions of "extremely important" and "very important" ratings of information services and facilities that were rated by 30 or more visitor groups.

- The services and facilities receiving the highest combined proportions of "extremely important" and "very important" ratings were:

  90% Park brochure/map
  89% Park interpretive pamphlets
  86% Park website

- Table 16 shows the importance ratings of each service and facility.

- The service/facility receiving the highest "not important" rating that was rated by 30 or more visitor groups was:

  3% Park newspaper *Boardwalk Talk*

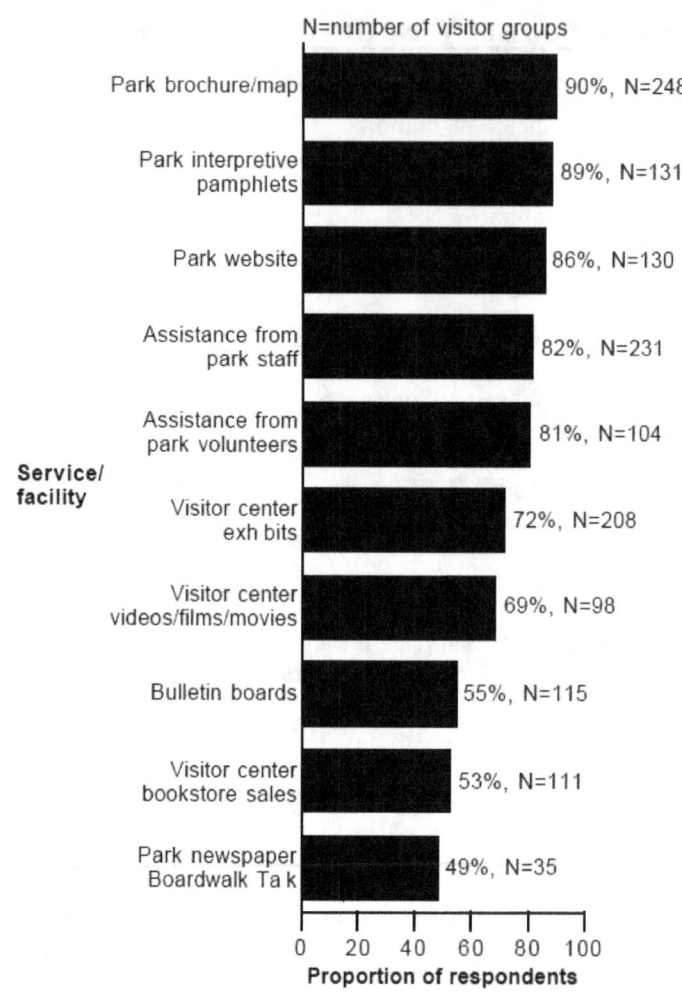

N=number of visitor groups

Service/facility	
Park brochure/map	90%, N=248
Park interpretive pamphlets	89%, N=131
Park website	86%, N=130
Assistance from park staff	82%, N=231
Assistance from park volunteers	81%, N=104
Visitor center exhibits	72%, N=208
Visitor center videos/films/movies	69%, N=98
Bulletin boards	55%, N=115
Visitor center bookstore sales	53%, N=111
Park newspaper Boardwalk Talk	49%, N=35

Proportion of respondents

Figure 52. Combined proportions of "extremely important" and "very important" ratings of information services and facilities

Table 16. Importance ratings of information services and facilities
(N=number of visitor groups)

Service/facility	N	Rating (%)*				
		Not important	Somewhat important	Moderately important	Very important	Extremely important
Assistance from park staff	231	0	3	15	42	40
Assistance from park volunteers	104	0	5	14	36	45
Bulletin boards	115	0	7	38	29	26
Junior Ranger program – **CAUTION!**	13	8	8	15	8	62
Park brochure/map	248	0	2	8	26	64
Park interpretive pamphlets	131	1	2	8	38	51
Park newspaper *Boardwalk Talk*	35	3	20	29	26	23
Park website (nps.gov/cong)	130	1	1	12	38	48
Ranger-led talks/ programs/walks – **CAUTION!**	20	0	5	10	20	65
Ranger-guided canoe tours – **CAUTION!**	6	0	17	0	33	50
Visitor center bookstore sales items	111	1	21	25	33	20
Visitor center videos/films/movies	98	0	8	23	32	37
Visitor center exhibits	208	0	7	22	35	37

Quality ratings of information services and facilities

Question 16c

For only those services and facilities that you or your personal group used, please rate their quality from 1-5.

1=Very poor
2=Poor
3=Average
4=Good
5=Very good

Results

- Figure 53 shows the combined proportions of "very good" and "good" ratings of information services and facilities that were rated by 30 or more visitor groups.

- The services and facilities receiving the highest combined proportions of "very good" and "good" ratings were:

  97% Assistance from park staff
  94% Assistance from park volunteers
  90% Park interpretive pamphlets

- Table 17 shows the quality ratings of each service and facility.

- The services/facilities receiving the highest "not important" rating that was rated by 30 or more visitor groups were:

  1% Park website
  1% Visitor center videos/films/movies

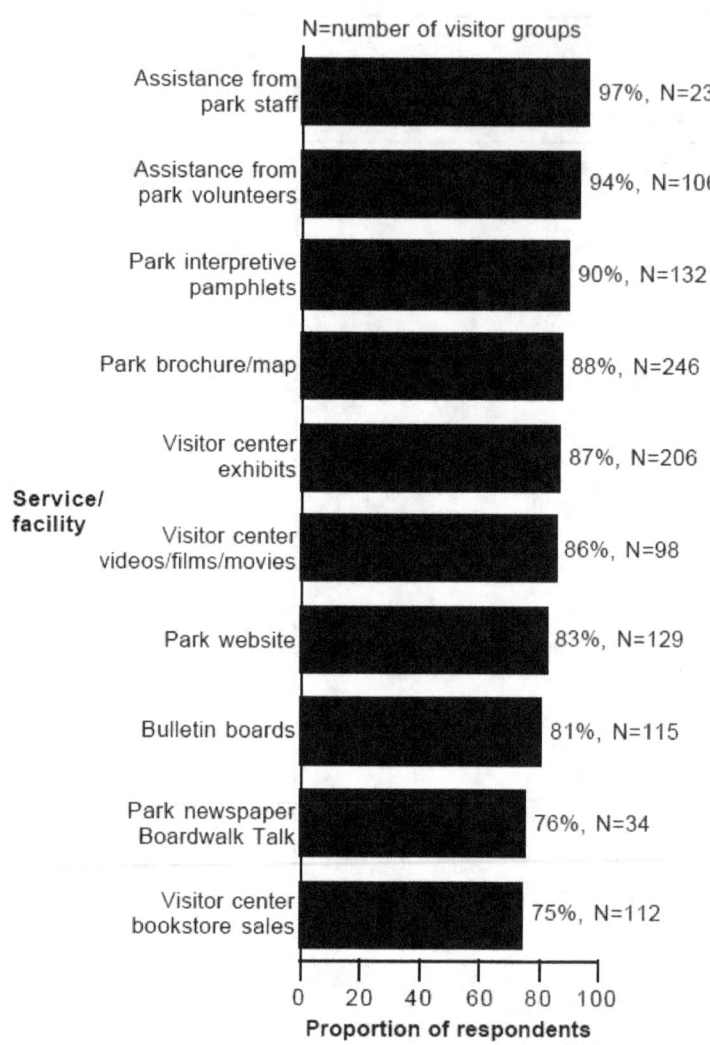

Figure 53. Combined proportions of "very good" and "good" ratings of information services and facilities

Table 17. Quality ratings of information services and facilities
(N=number of visitor groups that rated each service and facility)

Service/facility	N	Rating (%)*				
		Very Poor	Poor	Average	Good	Very good
Assistance from park staff	231	0	1	3	16	81
Assistance from park volunteers	106	0	1	6	22	72
Bulletin boards	115	0	0	19	36	45
Junior Ranger program – **CAUTION!**	12	0	0	17	33	50
Park brochure/map	246	0	1	11	33	55
Park interpretive pamphlets	132	0	1	9	34	56
Park newspaper *Boardwalk Talk*	34	0	3	21	41	35
Park website (nps.gov/cong)	129	1	2	15	42	41
Ranger-led talks/ programs/walks – **CAUTION!**	18	0	0	6	11	83
Ranger-guided canoe tours – **CAUTION!**	5	0	0	20	0	80
Visitor center bookstore sales items	112	0	3	22	32	43
Visitor center videos/films/movies	98	1	1	12	42	44
Visitor center exhibits	206	0	<1	13	32	55

Mean scores of importance and quality ratings of information services and facilities

- Figures 54 and 55 show the mean scores of importance and quality ratings of information and facilities that were rated by 30 or more visitor groups.

- All information services and facilities were rated above average.

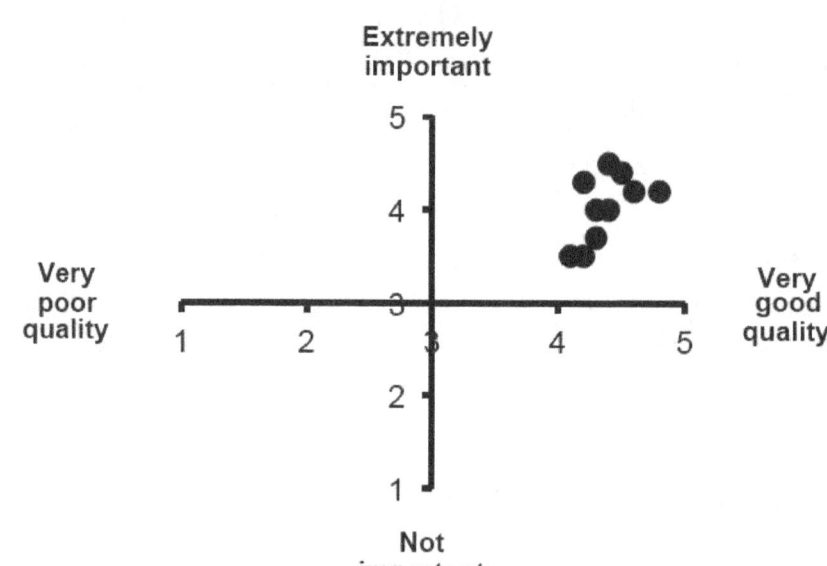

Figure 54. Mean scores of importance and quality ratings of information services and facilities

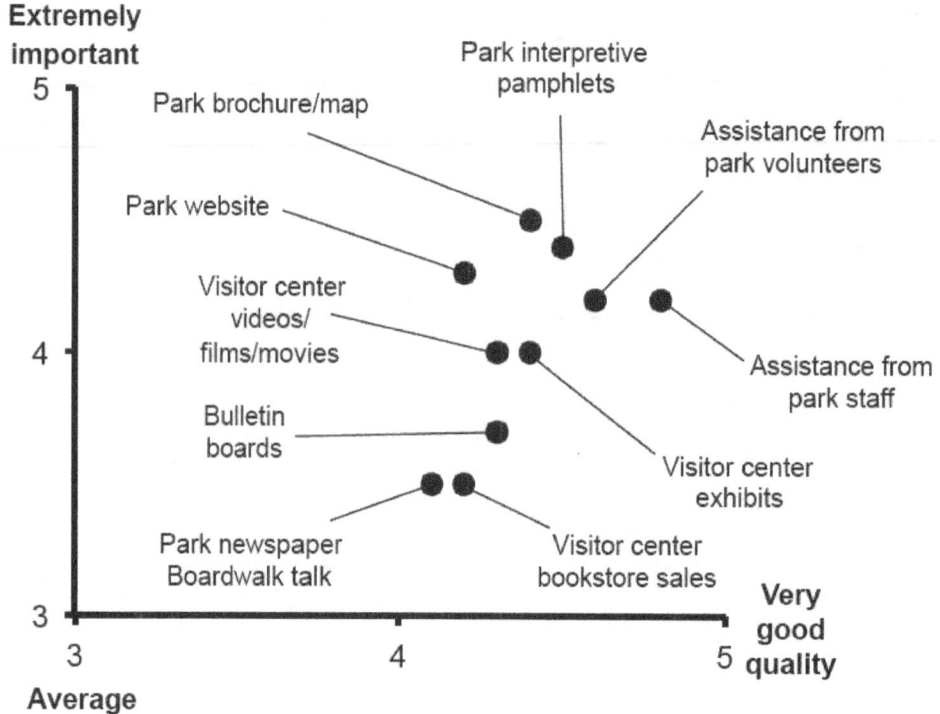

Figure 55. Detail of Figure 54

Visitor services and facilities used

Question 17a

Please indicate all of the visitor services and facilities that you or your personal group used at Congaree NP during this visit.

Results

- As shown in Figure 56, the most common visitor services and facilities used by visitor groups were:

   89% Boardwalks
   88% Restrooms
   85% Parking areas

- The least used service/facility was:

   3% Backcountry camping

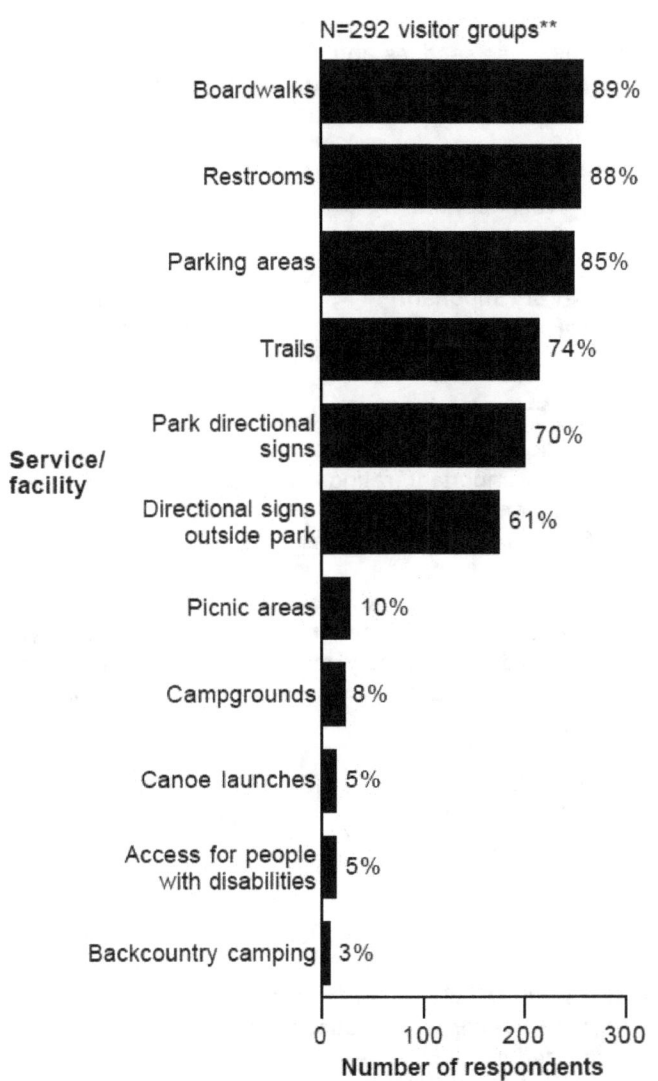

Figure 56. Visitor services and facilities used

Importance ratings of visitor services and facilities

Question 17b

For only those services and facilities that you or your personal group used, please rate their importance to your visit from 1-5.

1=Not important
2=Somewhat important
3=Moderately important
4=Very important
5=Extremely important

Results

- Figure 57 shows the combined proportions of "extremely important" and "very important" ratings of visitor services and facilities that were rated by 30 or more visitor groups.

- The visitor services and facilities receiving the highest combined proportions of "extremely important" and "very important" ratings were:

    97% Trails
    90% Park directional signs
    87% Directional signs outside park
    87% Boardwalks

- Table 18 shows the importance ratings of each service and facility.

- The service/facility receiving the highest "not important" ratings that was rated by 30 or more visitor groups was:

    1% Directional signs outside of park

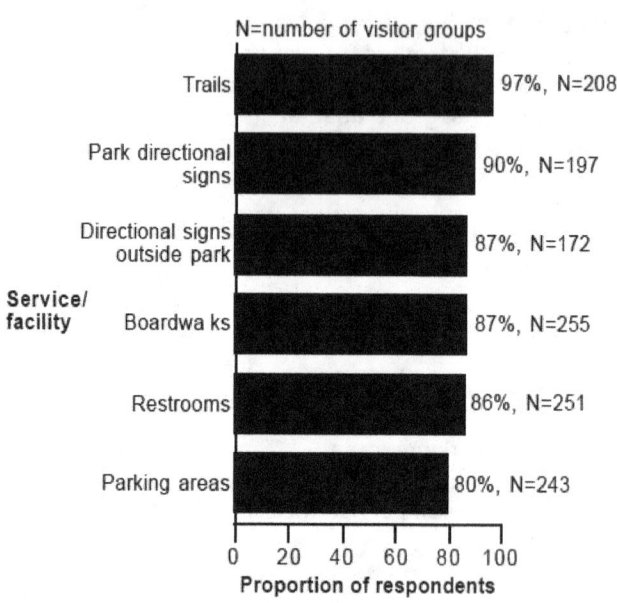

Figure 57. Combined proportions of "extremely important" and "very important" ratings of visitor services and facilities

Table 18. Importance ratings of visitor services and facilities
(N=number of visitor groups)

Service/facility	N	Rating (%)*				
		Not important	Somewhat important	Moderately important	Very important	Extremely important
Access for people with disabilities – **CAUTION!**	15	0	0	0	20	80
Backcountry camping – **CAUTION!**	9	0	0	0	44	56
Boardwalks	255	0	2	11	29	58
Campgrounds – **CAUTION!**	23	0	0	13	17	70
Canoe launches – **CAUTION!**	16	0	0	13	25	63
Directional signs outside of park	172	1	2	11	25	62
Park directional signs	197	0	2	8	30	60
Parking areas	243	0	6	14	32	48
Picnic areas – **CAUTION!**	29	0	3	21	48	28
Restrooms	251	0	2	12	21	65
Trails	208	<1	0	2	16	81

Quality ratings of visitor services and facilities

Question 17c

For only those services and facilities that you or your personal group used, please rate their quality from 1-5.

1=Very poor
2=Poor
3=Average
4=Good
5=Very good

Results

- Figure 58 shows the combined proportions of "very good" and "good" ratings of visitor services and facilities that were rated by 30 or more visitor groups.

- The services and facilities receiving the highest combined proportions of "very good" and "good" ratings were:

  97% Boardwalks
  95% Trails
  94% Restrooms

- Table 19 shows the quality ratings of each service and facility.

- The service/facility receiving the highest "very poor" rating that was rated by 30 or more visitor groups was:

  2% Directional signs outside of park

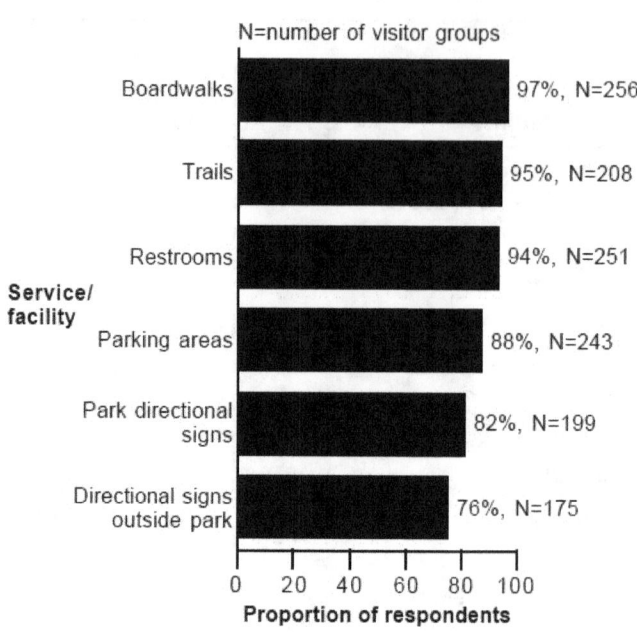

Figure 58. Combined proportions of "very good" and "good" ratings of visitor services and facilities

Table 19. Quality ratings of visitor services and facilities
(N=number of visitor groups that rated each service and facility)

Service/facility	N	Rating (%)*				
		Very poor	Poor	Average	Good	Very good
Access for people with disabilities – **CAUTION!**	15	0	7	0	20	73
Backcountry camping – **CAUTION!**	9	0	0	22	44	33
Boardwalks	256	0	<1	3	22	75
Campgrounds – **CAUTION!**	23	9	9	13	26	43
Canoe launches – **CAUTION!**	16	6	13	25	25	31
Directional signs outside of park	175	2	7	15	33	43
Park directional signs	199	1	2	15	33	49
Parking areas	243	0	1	11	26	62
Picnic areas – **CAUTION!**	28	0	0	11	39	50
Restrooms	251	<1	<1	5	22	72
Trails	208	<1	<1	4	27	68

Mean scores of importance and quality ratings of visitor services and facilities

- Figures 59 and 60 show the mean scores of importance and quality ratings of visitor services and facilities that were rated by 30 or more visitor groups.

- All visitor services and facilities were rated above average.

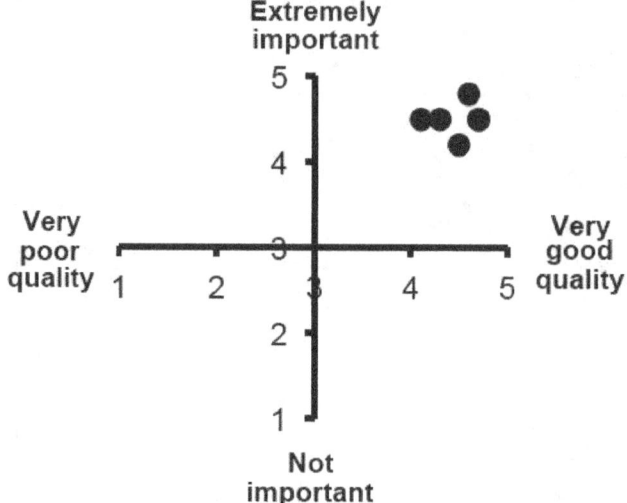

Figure 59. Mean scores of importance and quality of visitor services and facilities

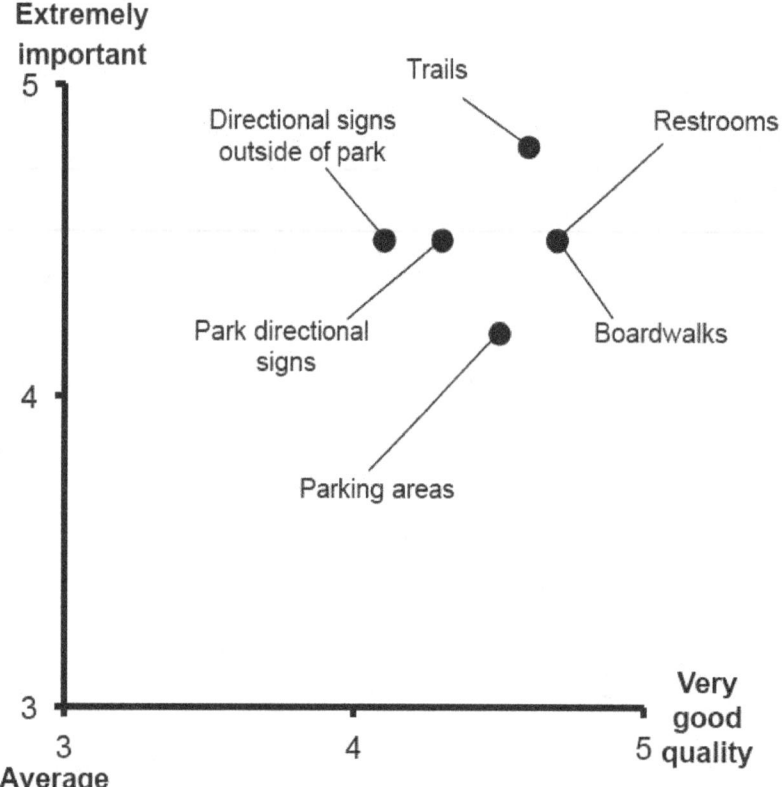

Figure 60. Detail of Figure 59

Importance of protecting park resources and attributes

Question 14

It is the National Park Service's responsibility to protect Congaree NP natural, scenic, and cultural resources while at the same time providing for public enjoyment. How important is protection of the following resources/attributes in the park to you and your personal group?

1=Not important
2=Somewhat important
3=Moderately important
4=Very important
5=Extremely important

Results

- As shown in Figure 61, the highest combined proportions of "extremely important" and "very important" ratings of protecting park resources and attributes included:

  94% Natural quiet/sounds of nature
  94% Clean air
  93% Clean water

- Table 20 shows the importance ratings of each resource/attribute

- The resource/attribute receiving the highest "not important" rating was:

  7% clear night sky (star gazing)

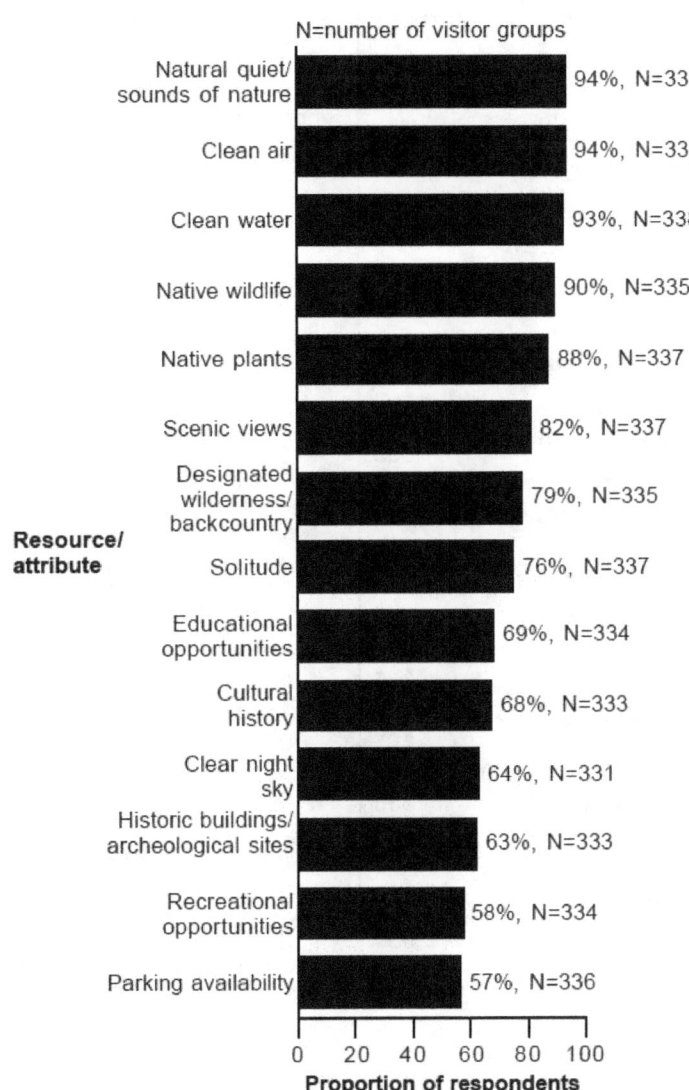

Figure 61. Combined proportions of "extremely important" and "very important" ratings of protecting park resources and attributes

Table 20. Importance of protecting park resources and attributes
(N=number of visitor groups that rated each resource/attribute)

Resource/attribute	N	Rating (%)*				
		Not important	Somewhat important	Moderately important	Very important	Extremely important
Clean air (visibility)	337	1	2	3	35	59
Clean water	338	1	1	4	34	59
Clear night sky (star gazing)	331	7	8	22	30	34
Cultural history (photographs/artifacts/ oral histories)	333	1	7	25	40	28
Designated wilderness/ backcountry	335	2	4	14	34	45
Educational opportunities	334	2	6	23	40	29
Historic buildings/ archeological sites	333	2	9	25	37	26
Native plants	337	<1	2	10	37	51
Native wildlife	335	0	1	8	36	54
Natural quiet/sounds of nature	337	0	1	6	30	64
Parking availability	336	1	10	31	38	19
Recreational opportunities	334	3	10	30	37	21
Scenic views	337	0	4	14	38	44
Solitude	337	2	4	18	33	43

Elements that affected park experience

Question 29
Please indicate how the following elements may have affected you and your personal group's park experience during this visit to Congaree NP?

Results
- Table 21 shows that the element that detracted from the greatest number of visitor groups' experience was airplane noise (42%).

- The element that added the most to visitor experiences was encountering small numbers of visitors on the trail (39%).

- "Other" elements that added to and detracted from visitor groups' experience are shown in Tables 22 and 23.

Table 21. Effects of different elements on the park experience
N=number of visitors groups that responded to the question
n_1 = number of visitor groups that rated each element
n_2 = number of visitor groups that did not experience each element

Element	Total N	Rating (%)*				Did not experience	
		n_1	Detracted from	No effect	Added to	n_2	% of total
Airplane noise	326	131	42	57	<1	195	60
Automobile noise	328	92	14	86	0	236	72
Gunshots from neighboring lands	327	68	32	65	3	259	79
Noise from park staff activities	326	75	13	87	0	251	77
Train noise	326	64	16	81	3	262	80
Other visitors' activities	324	230	12	84	4	94	29
Small number of visitors on trails	325	291	3	57	39	34	10
Large number of visitors on trails	324	90	28	71	1	234	72
Small number of visitors canoeing/kayaking	323	56	2	63	36	267	83
Large number of visitors canoeing/kayaking	320	33	9	82	9	287	90
Impact of wild pigs	325	124	30	40	30	201	62
Other	87	34	41	24	35	53	61

Table 22. "Other" elements that added to visitor groups' experiences
(N= 14 comments; some visitor groups made more than one comment)

Element	Number of times mentioned
Sounds	2
Beautiful surroundings	1
Bird noise	1
Bird sightings	1
Friendly staff	1
Owls	1
Park staff/volunteers	1
Smell of woods	1
Snake sightings	1
Warm weather	1
Wild pig sightings	1
Wildlife	1
Woodpecker	1

Table 23. "Other" elements that detracted from visitor groups' experiences
(N= 16 comments; some visitor groups made more than one comment)

Element	Number of times mentioned
Visitors with dogs	3
Campground facilities	2
Hard time finding trails and directions at times	1
Lack of canoe program	1
Litter	1
Not enough staff	1
Not enough wild pigs	1
Outhouses at campground	1
Poor signage	1
Rain	1
Slippery mud	1
Unable to use boardwalk - too hot to leave dogs in car	1
Unexpected water on Oakridge Trail	1

Expenditures

Total expenditures inside and outside the park

Question 26

For you and your personal group, please estimate all expenditures for the items listed below for this visit to Congaree NP and the surrounding area (within 1-hour drive of the park).

Results

- 65% of visitor groups spent $1-$200 (see Figure 62).

- 12% spent $201-$400.

- The average visitor group expenditure was $153.

- The median group expenditure (50% of groups spent more and 50% of groups spent less) was $55.

- The average total expenditure per person (per capita) was $74.

- As shown in Figure 63, the largest proportions of total expenditures inside and outside the park were:

    30% Lodges, hotels, motels, cabins, B&B, etc.
    22% Gas and oil
    22% Restaurants and bars

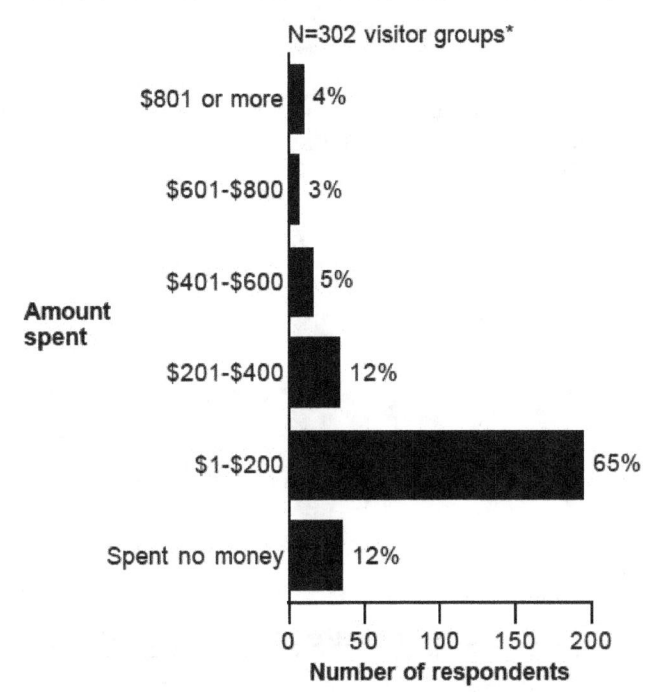

Figure 62. Total expenditures inside and outside the park

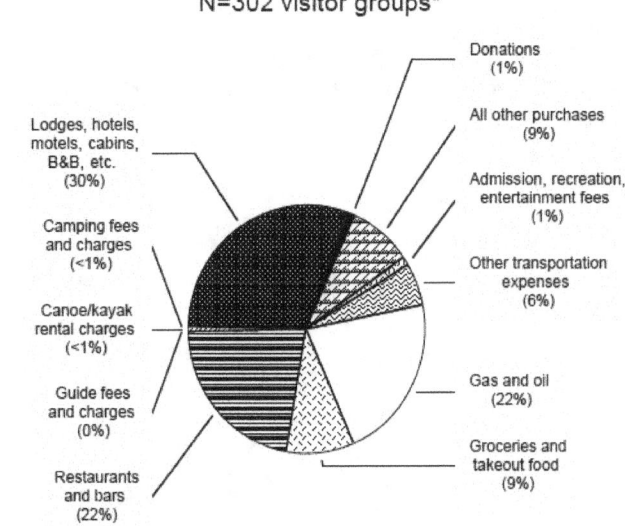

Figure 63. Proportions of total expenditures inside and outside the park

Number of adults covered by expenditures

Question 26c
How many adults (18 years or older)
do these expenses cover?

Results
- 64% of visitor groups had two
  adults covered by expenditures
  (see Figure 64).

- 18% had one adult covered by
  expenditures.

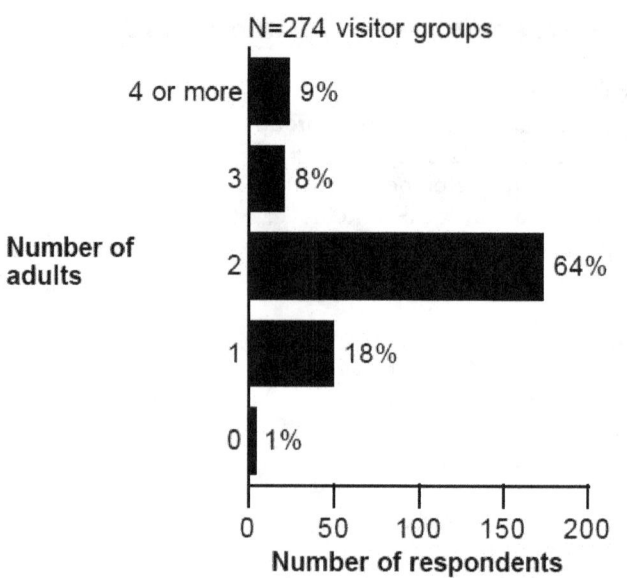

Figure 64. Number of adults covered by expenditures

Number of children covered by expenditures

Question 26c
How many children (under 18
years) do these expenses cover?

Results
- 85% of visitor groups had no
  children covered by expenditures
  (see Figure 65).

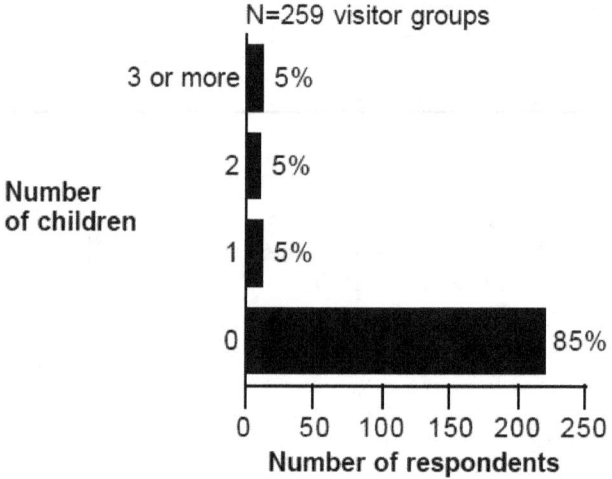

Figure 65. Number of children covered by expenditures

Expenditures inside the park

Question 26a

Please list your personal group's total expenditures inside Congaree NP.

Results

- 45% of visitor groups spent no money inside the park (see Figure 66).

- 37% spent $1-$25

- The average visitor group expenditure inside the park was $13.

- The median group expenditure (50% groups spent more and 50% of groups spent less) was $3.

- The average total expenditure per person (per capita) was $11.

- As shown in Figure 67, the largest proportion of total expenditures inside the park was:

  76% All other purchases

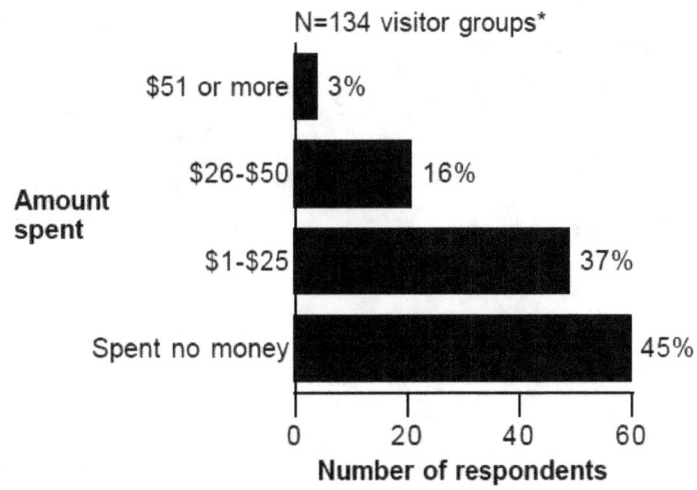

Figure 66. Total expenditures inside the park

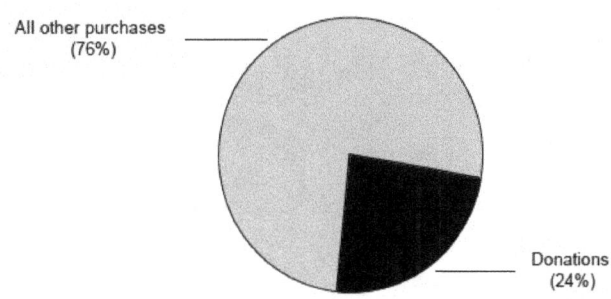

Figure 67. Proportions of total expenditures inside the park

All other purchases (souvenirs, film, books, sporting goods, clothing, etc.)

- 45% of visitor groups spent no money on other purchases inside the park (see Figure 68).

- 38% spent $1-$25.

- 16% spent $26-$50.

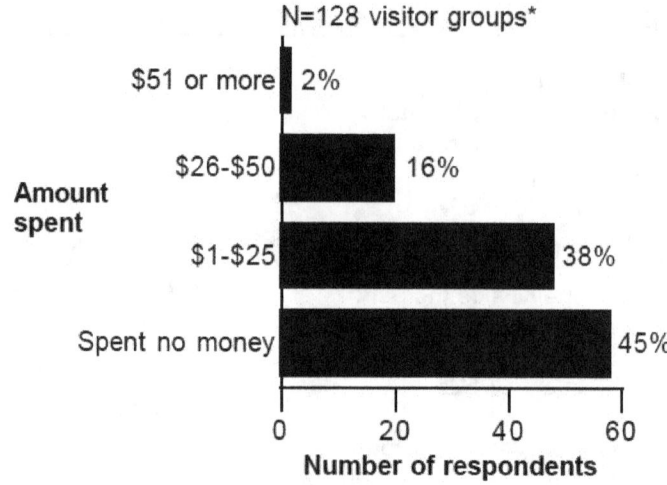

Figure 68. Expenditures for all other purchases inside the park

Donations

- 80% of visitor groups spent no money on donations inside the park (see Figure 69).

- 15% spent $1-$10.

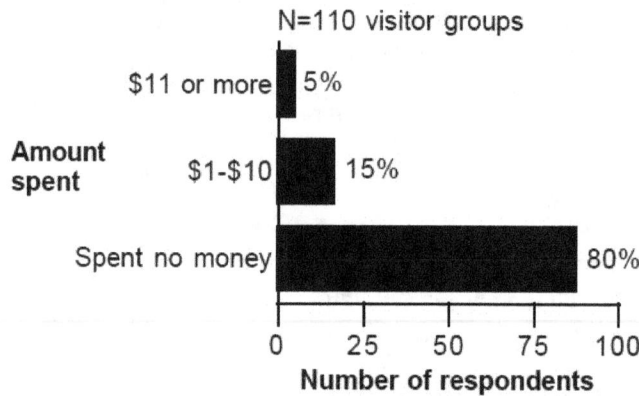

Figure 69. Expenditures for donations inside the park

Expenditures outside the park

Question 26b
Please list your personal group's total expenditures in the surrounding area outside the park (within 1-hour drive of park).

Results
- 63% of visitor groups spent $1-$200 in the surrounding area outside the park (see Figure 70).

- 14% spent no money.

- The average visitor group expenditure outside the park was $150.

- The median group expenditure (50% groups spent more and 50% of groups spent less) was $50.

- The average total expenditure per person (per capita) was $79.

- As shown in Figure 71, the largest proportions of total expenditures outside the park were:

    31% Lodges, hotels, motels, cabins, B&B, etc.
    23% Gas and oil
    23% Restaurants and bars

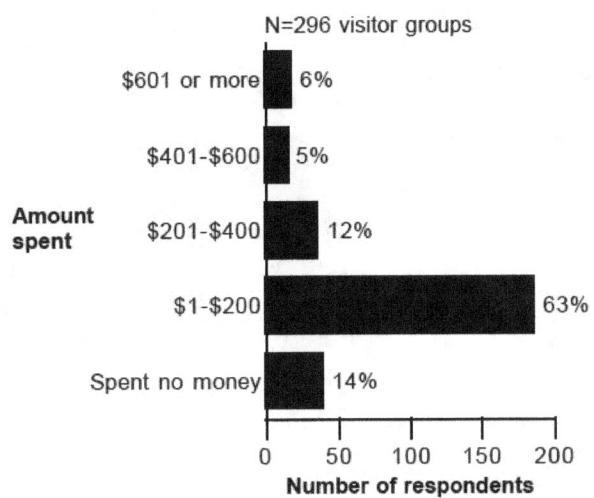

Figure 70. Total expenditures outside the park within a 1-hour drive

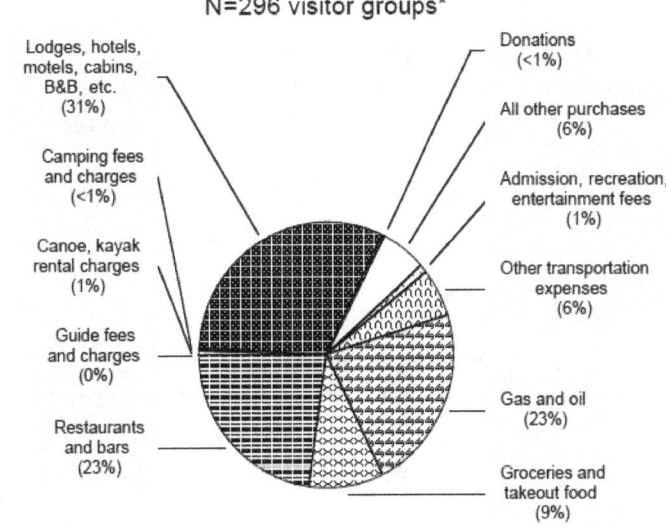

Figure 71. Proportions of total expenditures outside the park within a 1-hour drive

<u>Lodges, hotels, motels, cabins, B&B, etc.</u>

- 66% of visitor groups spent no money on lodging outside the park (see Figure 72).

- 14% spent $1-$100.

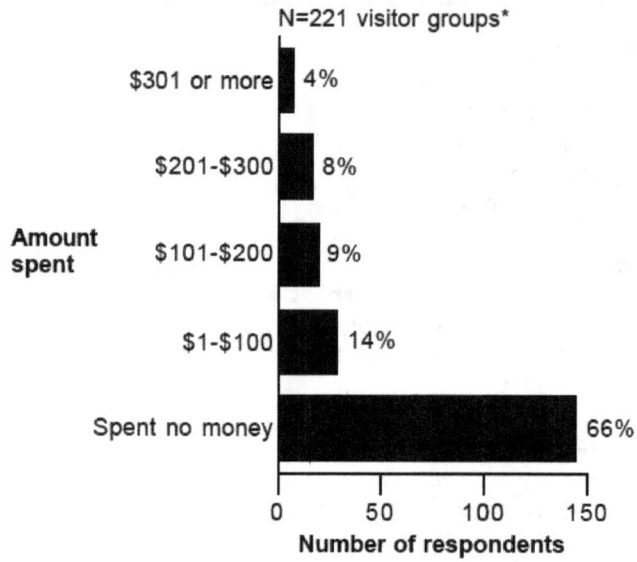

Figure 72. Expenditures for lodging outside the park

<u>Camping fees and charges</u>

- 98% of visitor groups spent no money on camping fees and charges outside the park (see Figure 73).

- 2% spent $1-$50.

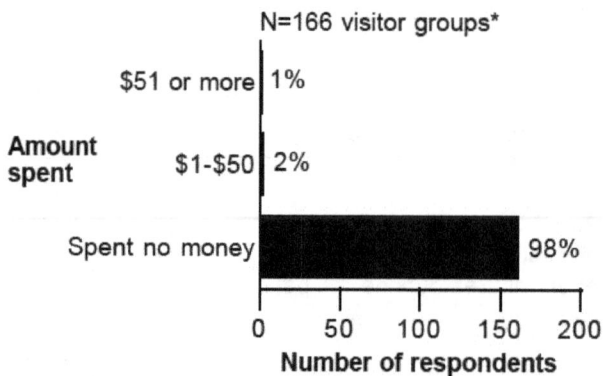

Figure 73. Expenditures for camping fees and charges outside the park

Canoe/kayak rental charges

- 98% of visitor groups spent no money on canoe/kayak rental charges outside the park (see Figure 74).

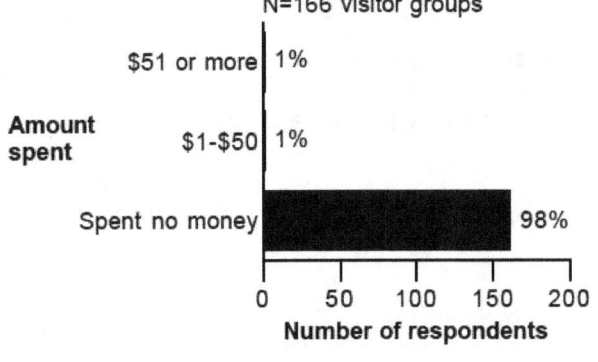

Figure 74. Expenditures for canoe/kayak rental charges outside the park

Guide fees and charges

- 100% of visitor groups spent no money on guide fees and charges outside the park (see Figure 75).

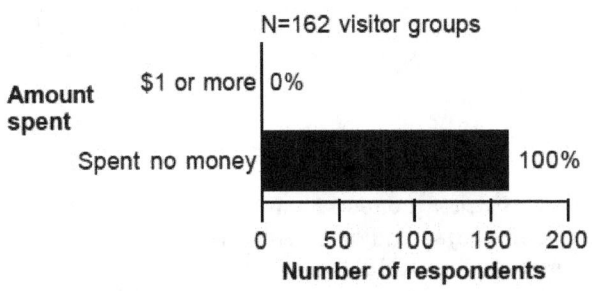

Figure 75. Expenditures for guide fees and charges outside the park

Restaurants and bars

- 44% of visitor groups spent no money on restaurants and bars outside the park (see Figure 76).

- 37% spent $1-$50.

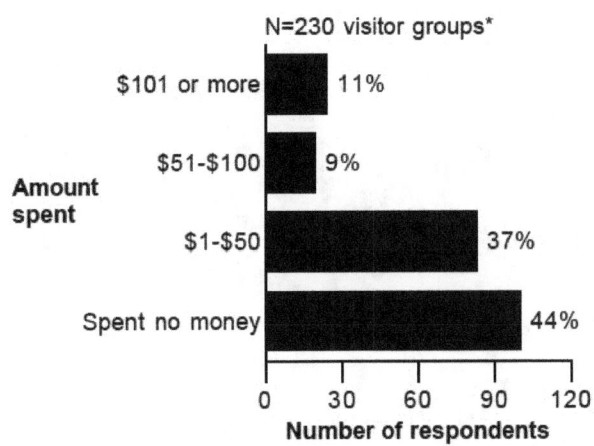

Figure 76. Expenditures for restaurants and bars outside the park

Groceries and takeout food

- 56% of visitor groups spent no money on groceries and takeout food outside the park (see Figure 77).

- 35% spent $1-$50.

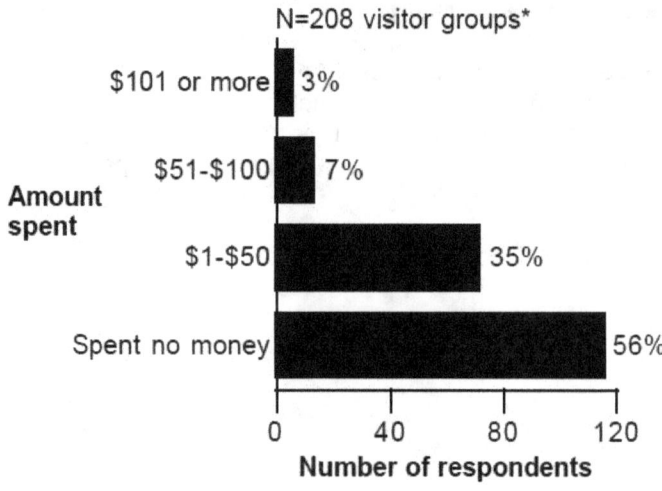

Figure 77. Expenditures for groceries and takeout food outside the park

Gas and oil (auto, RV, boat, etc.)

- 60% of visitor groups spent $1-$50 on gas and oil outside the park (see Figure 78).

- 18% spent $51-$100.

- 18% spent no money.

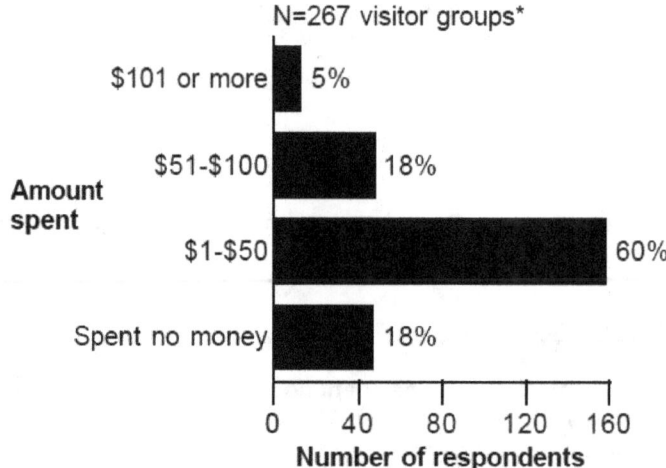

Figure 78. Expenditures for gas and oil outside the park

Other transportation (rental cars, taxis, auto repairs, but NOT airfare)

- 92% of visitor groups spent no money on other transportation outside the park (see Figure 79).

- 5% spent $51 or more.

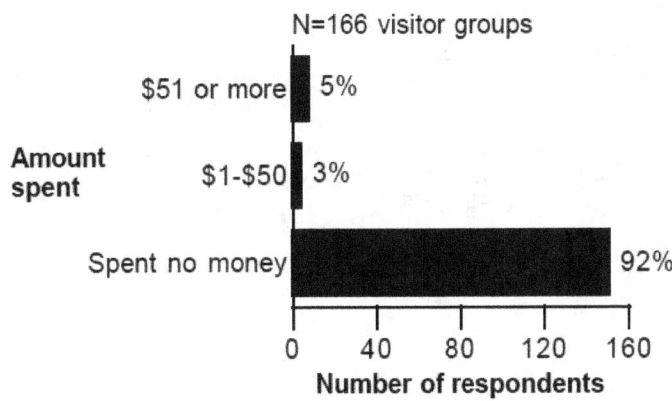

Figure 79. Expenditures for other transportation outside the park

Admission, recreation and entertainment fees

- 90% of visitor groups spent no money on admission, recreation and entertainment fees outside the park (see Figure 80).

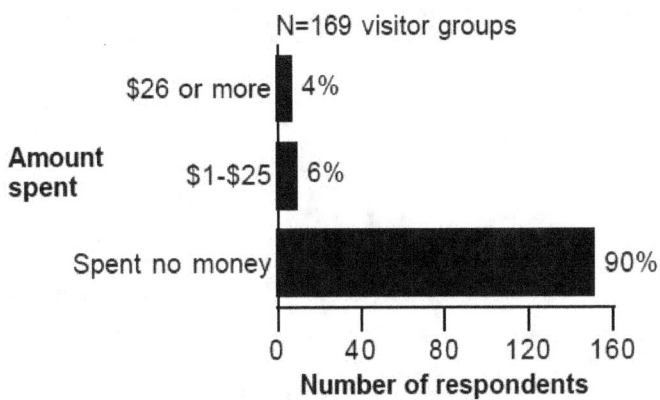

Figure 80. Expenditures for admission, recreation, and entertainment fees outside the park

All other purchases (souvenirs, film, books, sporting goods, clothing, etc.)

- 76% of visitor groups spent no money on all other purchases outside the park (see Figure 81).

- 17% spent $1-$50.

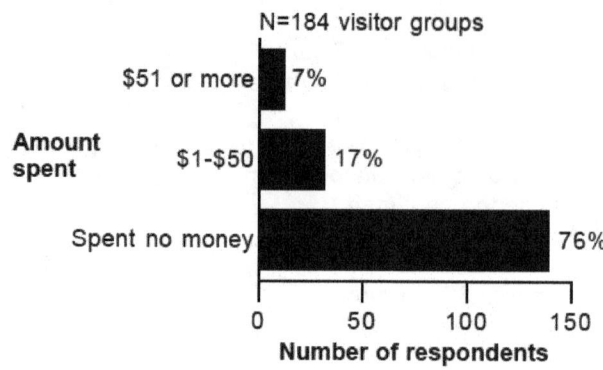

Figure 81. Expenditures for all other purchases outside the park

Donations

- 92% of visitor groups spent no money on donations outside the park (see Figure 82).

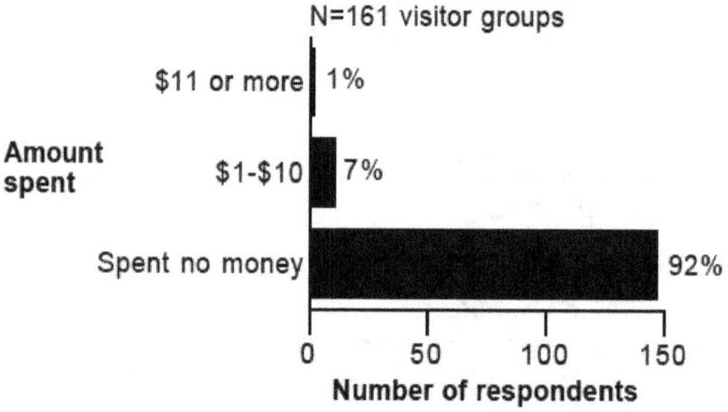

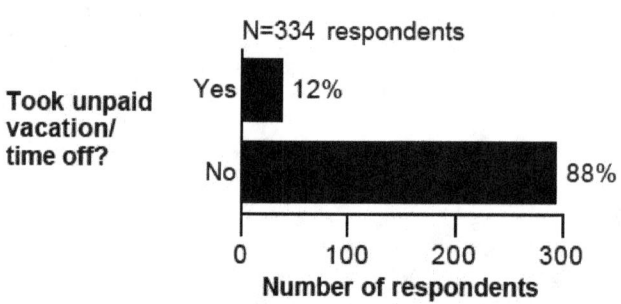

Figure 82. Expenditures for donations outside the park

Unpaid vacation/unpaid time off

Question 25c
Did your household take any unpaid vacation or take unpaid time off of work to come on this trip?

Results
- 12% of respondents took unpaid vacation or unpaid time off work to come on this trip (see Figure 83).

N=334 respondents

Took unpaid vacation/ time off?
Yes 12%
No 88%

Number of respondents

Figure 83. Respondents that took unpaid vacation/ unpaid time off to come on this trip

Preferences for Future Visits

Likelihood of future visit

Question 28

Would you and your group be likely to visit Congaree NP again in the future?

Results

- 81% of visitor groups indicated that they would be likely to visit Congaree NP again in the future (see Figure 84).

- 17% were not sure about visiting the park in the future.

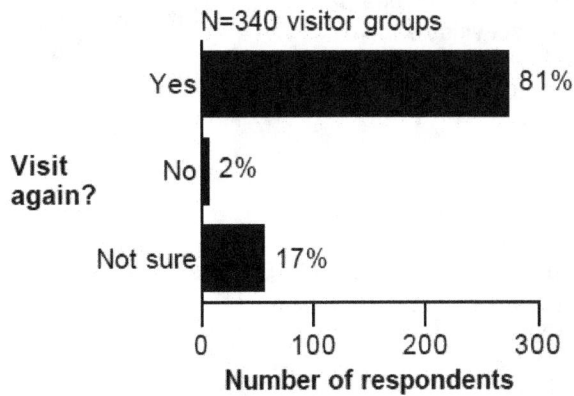

Figure 84. Visitor groups that would likely visit Congaree NP in the future

Preferred activities and programs on future visits

Question 30

If you were to visit Congaree NP in the future, which types of organized activities and programs would you and your personal group like to have available?

Results

- 84% of visitor groups were interested in attending organized activities or programs on a future visit to the park (see Figure 85).

- As shown in Figure 86, of those visitor groups that wanted organized activities/programs, the most preferred were:

  68% Canoeing/kayaking
  57% Owl prowls
  57% Night walk/night sky program

- "Other" activities/programs (7%) were:

  Biking trails
  Citizen science
  Dog-friendly walk
  Firefly walks
  Canoe/kayak rentals
  Guided hikes off-trail when snakes are not active
  Hiking
  Include leashed dogs
  More technical exhibits in visitor center
  Narrated boat tour
  Research lectures
  Technical presentations
  Trails open to mountain biking
  Tree and plant identification
  Tree top tour
  Video about the park and region

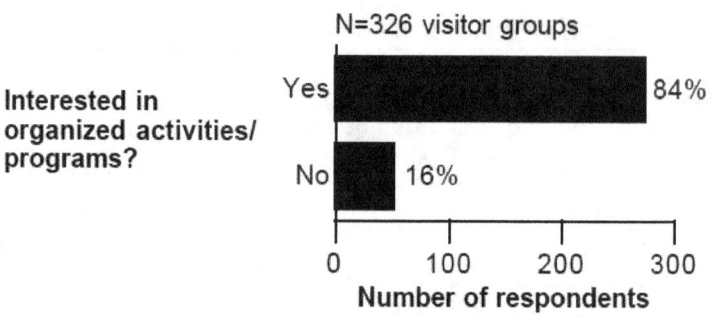

Figure 85. Visitor groups interested in activities and programs

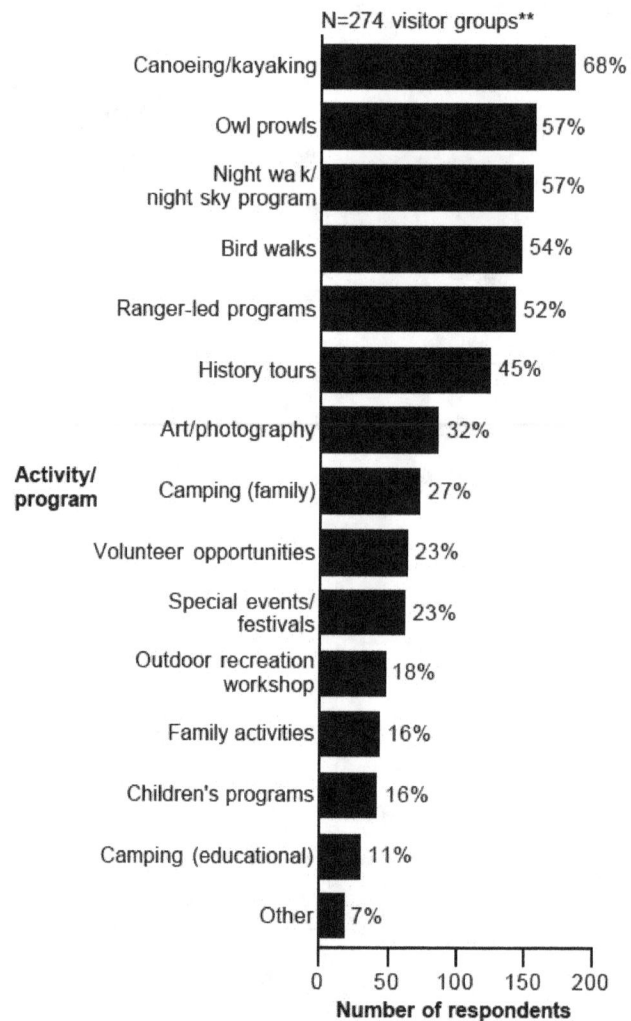

Figure 86. Preferred activities and programs

Preferred topics to learn on future visits

Question 31

If you were to visit Congaree NP in the future, which subjects would you and your personal group like to learn about?

Results

- 93% of visitor groups were interested in learning about the park on future visits (see Figure 87).

- As shown in Figure 88, of those visitor groups that were interested in learning about the park, the most common subjects were:

  - 74% Plants/animals
  - 61% Champion trees
  - 61% Old growth floodplain forest

- No "other" subjects (1%) were specified.

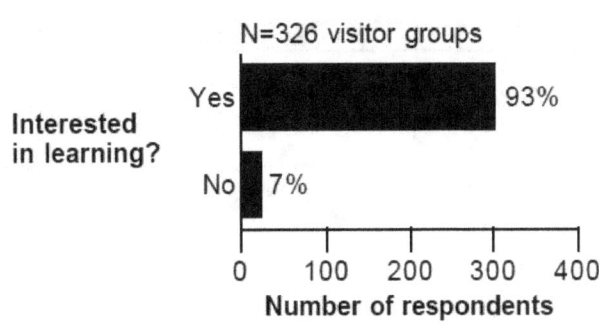

Figure 87. Visitor groups that were interested in learning about the park

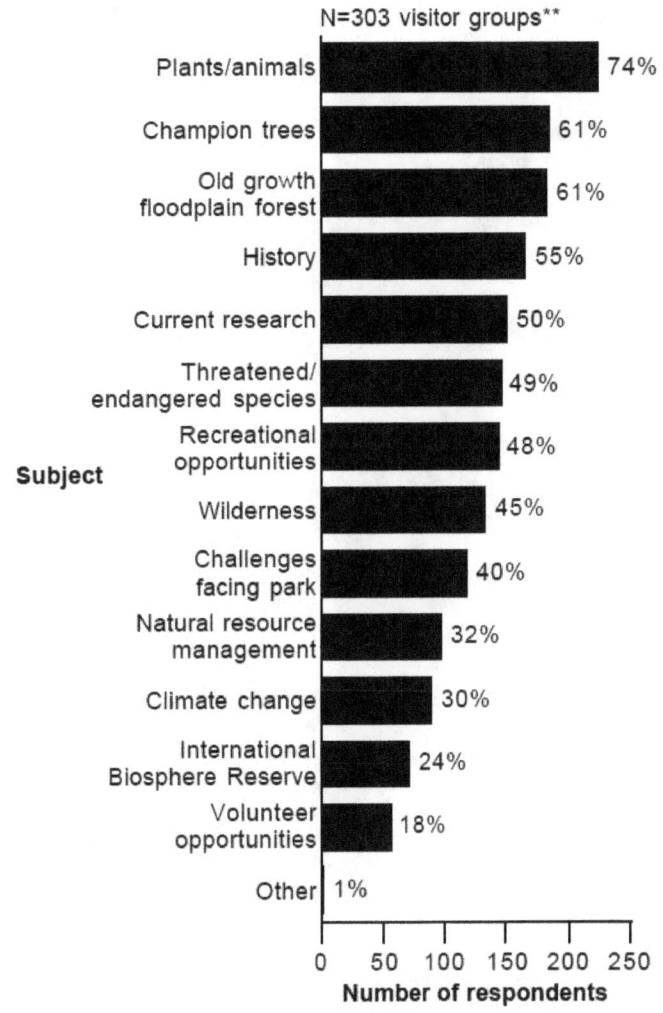

Figure 88. Subjects to learn on a future visit

Overall Quality

Quality of facilities, services, and recreational opportunities

Question 27

Overall, how would you rate the quality of facilities, services, and recreational opportunities provided to you and your personal group at Congaree NP during this visit?

Results

- 97% of visitor groups rated the overall quality of facilities, services, and recreational opportunities as "very good" or "good" (see Figure 89).

- 1% rated the quality as "poor."

- No visitor groups rated the quality as "very poor."

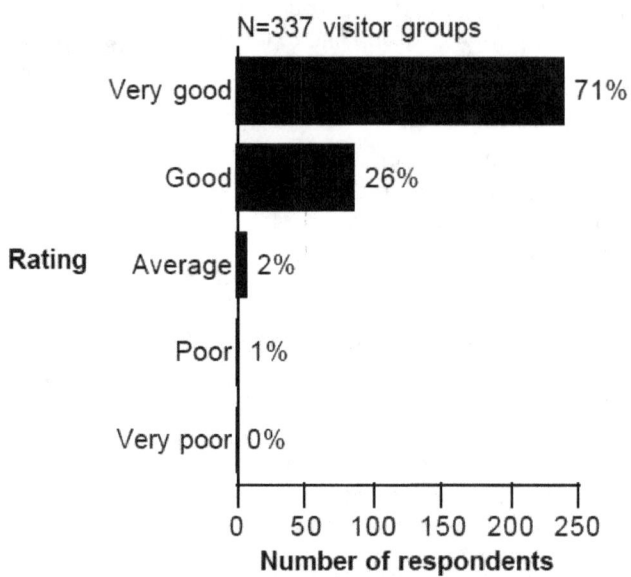

Figure 89. Overall quality rating of facilities, services, and recreational opportunities

Visitor Comment Summaries

What visitors liked most

Question 32a
What did you and your personal group like most about your visit to Congaree NP? (Open-ended)

Results
- 91% of visitor groups (N=310) responded to this question.

- Table 24 shows a summary of visitor comments. The transcribed open-ended comments can be found in the Visitor Comments section.

Table 24. What visitors liked most
(N=597 comments; some visitor groups made more than one comment)

Comment	Number of times mentioned
PERSONNEL (7%)	
Friendliness/helpfulness of park staff/volunteers	19
Park staff	8
Knowledgeable staff/volunteers	5
Talking with staff and volunteers	4
Outstanding interactions with staff	2
Other comment	1
INTERPRETIVE SERVICES (7%)	
Brochures	5
Self-guided tours	5
Educational	4
Guided tours	4
Trail markers	4
Film	3
Visitor center	3
Canoe trip	2
History	2
Information	2
Junior Ranger program	2
Maps	2
Other comments	5
FACILITIES/MAINTENANCE (19%)	
Boardwalk	53
Trails	38
Cleanliness	7
Well-marked trails	5
Boardwalks were well-maintained	3
Bridges	2
Other comments	8

Table 24. What visitors liked most (continued)

Comment	Number of times mentioned
POLICY MANAGEMENT (4%)	
Not crowded	7
Fees	4
Wilderness	3
Free camping	2
Other comments	6
RESOURCE MANAGEMENT (22%)	
Trees	24
Big trees	13
Birds	11
Old growth forest	10
Cypress/cypress knees	8
Wildlife	7
Floodplain	6
Champion trees	5
Forest	5
Swamps	5
Clean/fresh air	4
Woodpeckers	4
Diversity	3
Flora	3
Loblolly pines	3
Wild pigs	3
Plants	2
Other comments	13
GENERAL (42%)	
Quiet	31
Solitude	32
Peace	20
Hiking	16
Beauty	13
Nature	9
Canoeing/kayaking	8
No bugs	7
Quiet hike	6
Accessibility	5
Camping	5
Outdoors	5
Weather	5
Scenery	4
Unique place	4
Beautiful day	3
Bird sounds	3
Interesting park	3

Table 24. What visitors liked most (continued)

Comment	Number of times mentioned
Atmosphere	2
Beautiful scenery	2
Beauty of the forest	2
Cedar Creek canoe/kayak trip	2
Everything	2
Exercise	2
Peaceful hike	2
Serenity	2
Sounds of nature	2
Other comments	51

What visitors liked least

Question 32b

What did you and your personal group like least about your visit to Congaree NP? (Open-ended)

Results

- 61% of visitor groups (N=207) responded to this question.

- Table 25 shows a summary of visitor comments. The transcribed open-ended comments can be found in the Visitor Comments section.

Table 25. What visitors liked least
(N=229 comments; some visitor groups made more than one comment)

Comment	Number of times mentioned
PERSONNEL (1%)	
Comments	2
INTERPRETIVE SERVICES (10%)	
Trail signage	6
Shortage of canoe tours	4
Lack of detailed information and education	3
Other comments	11
FACILITIES/MAINTENANCE (17%)	
Litter	7
Lack of drinking water	5
Lack of parking	3
Need bathhouse at campground	3
Not enough benches	3
Trail signage	3
Campgrounds need upgrading	2
More trails	2
Other comments	12
POLICY/MANAGEMENT (18%)	
Signage to the park	7
Airplane/train noise	6
Dogs not allowed	5
Disruptive children	4
Dogs in the park	4
Unable to kayak or canoe	2
Other comments	14
RESOURCE MANAGEMENT (10%)	
Did not see much wildlife	5
Impact of wild pigs	5
Dead trees	2
Did not see many plants blooming	2
Other comments	10

Table 25. What visitors liked least (continued)

Comment	Number of times mentioned
GENERAL (42%)	
Nothing to dislike	28
Liked it all	11
Not enough time	9
Rain	8
Mosquitos	4
Cold/cool weather	3
Great experience	3
Visitor survey	3
Lack of restaurants close to park	2
Other comments	26

Significance of the park

Question 33

Congaree NP was established because of its significance to the nation. In your opinion, what is the national significance of this park? (Open-ended)

Results

- 85% of visitor groups (N=289) responded to this question.

- Table 26 shows a summary of visitor comments. The transcribed comments can be found in the Visitor Comments section.

Table 26. Significance of the park
(N=401 comments; some visitor groups made more than one comment)

Comment	Number of times mentioned
Old growth forest	20
Unique environment	15
Example of old growth forest	10
Preserve/protect old growth forest	10
Big trees	9
Swamp	9
Floodplain	8
History of area	8
Trees	8
Old growth floodplain forest	7
Preserve/protect wilderness	7
Cypress trees/knees	6
Natural habitat	6
Preservation for historical purposes	6
Preserve/protect ecosystem	6
Preserve/protect for future	6
Unique/important ecosystem	6
Beauty	5
Biodiversity	5
Important	5
Old growth trees	5
Preservation of old growth floodplain forest	5
Champion trees	4
Conservation	4
Don't know/unsure	4
Exposure to unique area	4
Last stand of old growth forest	4
Natural setting	4
Preservation of nature	4
Preservation of unique/rare environment	4
Wetland environment	4
Accessibility of old growth floodplain forest	3
Biosphere	3
Last stand of old growth bottomland forest	3
Preservation	3

Table 26. Significance of the park (continued)

Comment	Number of times mentioned
Preservation of habitat	3
Preserve/protect trees	3
Preserve/protect wildlife	3
Trees	3
Unique habitat important for wildlife	3
Wildlife	3
Biodiversity	2
Demonstrates human impact	2
Demonstrates importance of nature	2
Ecosystem	2
Forest preservation/protection	2
Location of park	2
Natural heritage	2
Natural resources	2
Nature	2
Oldest old growth forest	2
Plants	2
Preservation of old growth trees	2
Quiet	2
Size of the forest	2
Very significant	2
Wilderness area	2
Other comments	131

Planning for the future

Question 34
If you were a manager planning for the future of Congaree NP, what would you and personal group propose? (Open-ended)

Results
- 62% of visitor groups (N=212) responded to this question.

- Table 27 shows a summary of visitor comments. The transcribed comments can be found in the Visitor Comments section.

Table 27. Planning for the future
(N=295 comments; some visitor groups made more than one comment)

Comment	Number of times mentioned
PERSONNEL (3%)	
Increase staff and volunteers	6
Other comments	3
INTERPRETIVE SERVICES (22%)	
Expand educational opportunities	9
Increase activities/recreation opportunities	8
Educate public about value of park and its resources	7
Improve/update website	4
Improve/update park video	3
More history	3
More information on plant and animal life	3
More programs	3
More ranger-led tours	3
Canopy tour	2
Improve interpretive signs on boardwalk	2
Other comments	21
FACILITIES/MAINTENANCE (26%)	
Expand trail system	14
Improve/expand campground facilities	8
More boardwalks	6
Improve/add trail signs/maps	5
More interpretive signs along the boardwalk	5
Add RV campground	4
Bike trails	4
Better signage	2
Boardwalk maintenance	2
Mileage on trail signs	2
More signage	2
Water at the camping areas	2
Other comments	22

Table 27. Planning for the future (continued)

Comment	Number of times mentioned
POLICY/MANAGEMENT (34%)	
Publicize park/activities	17
Expand park area	16
Continue to protect park/environment	14
Expand/improve kayak/canoeing activities	5
Add food/lodging	4
Improve directional signage to the park	4
Keep it as natural as possible	3
Add another entrance	2
Continue balancing recreation with resource protection	2
Coordinate with nearby resources	2
Do not over develop	2
Limit plane/train noise	2
Maintain/increase funding	2
More participation/outreach in local communities	2
Other comments	23
RESOURCE MANAGEMENT (3%)	
Eliminate wild pigs	4
Continue exotic species work	3
Other comments	3
GENERAL (10%)	
Keep it as it is	17
Keep up the good work	3
Everything was great	2
Other comments	8

Additional comments

Question 35
Is there anything else you and your personal group would like to tell us about your visit to Congaree NP (Open-ended)

Results
- 54% of visitor groups (N=184) responded to this question.

- Table 28 shows a summary of visitor comments. The transcribed comments can be found in the Visitor Comments section.

Table 28. Additional comments
(N=259 comments; some visitor groups made more than one comment.)

Comment	Number of times mentioned
PERSONNEL (23%)	
Park staff was helpful	24
Staff was great/excellent	15
Park staff was knowledgeable	8
Park staff was friendly/enthusiastic	6
Other comments	7
INTERPRETIVE SERVICES (7%)	
Improve information on exhibits	5
Other comments	12
FACILITIES/MAINTENANCE (12%)	
Enjoyed boardwalk	4
Great facilities	4
Improve accessibility of boardwalk maps, add mileage	2
Improve signage on trails	2
Very clean restrooms	2
Other comments	17
POLICY/MANAGEMENT (5%)	
More advertising	4
Leave it alone	3
Other comments	7
RESOURCE MANAGEMENT (1%)	
Comments	3

Table 28. Additional comments (continued)

GENERAL (52%)	
Great experience	26
Enjoyed visit	14
Will return	13
Love the park	12
Thank you	11
Great park/place	7
Beautiful park	6
Keep up the good work	5
It was a lot of fun	3
Love the mosquito meter	3
Interesting and unique park	2
Love the national parks	2
Love the swamp	2
Peaceful place	2
Other comments	26

Visitor Comments

This section contains visitor responses to open-ended questions.

Q32a. What did you and your personal group like most about your visit to Congaree NP?

- A chance to walk through old growth floodplain forest
- A perfect Sunday afternoon walk
- All of it was great, enjoyed it very much
- An interesting and different national park
- Animal life
- Areas of unaltered natural wilderness
- Atmosphere and hiking trails
- Beautiful and peaceful, welcoming rangers
- Beautiful day, fresh air, quiet
- Beautiful park, sound of woodpeckers, solitude, scenery, park staff
- Beautiful scenery
- Beautiful scenery
- Beautiful scenery and boardwalk
- Beautiful tall trees
- Beautiful weather, wonderful canoe trip
- Beauty of park
- Beauty of trees in park
- Being able to walk trails, friendliness/helpfulness of park staff
- Being outdoors with a nice trail and self-guided activities
- Being outdoors, trees, no mosquitos
- Being with family in nature
- Big trees, knees
- Birds, fauna, flora
- Birds, trees
- Boardwalk
- Boardwalk
- Boardwalk
- Boardwalk
- Boardwalk
- Boardwalk
- Boardwalk
- Boardwalk
- Boardwalk allowed us to get into the swamp and the self-guided boardwalk numbers/items were fascinating
- Boardwalk hikes
- Boardwalk signage
- Boardwalk trail
- Boardwalk trails self-guided tours
- Boardwalk, accompanied by educational map/trail markers

- Boardwalk, brochure, solitude
- Boardwalk, quiet, trees/nature
- Boardwalk, quietness, center
- Boardwalk, talk with ranger and volunteer
- Boardwalk, trails
- Boardwalk, trees
- Boardwalks
- Camping
- Canoe trail, staff at visitor center, and nice beach to camp on Congaree River
- Canoe trip and hiking
- Canoeing
- Canoeing Cedar Creek
- Cedar Creek kayak trip
- Champion trees, beauty of nature, lack of litter (trash), clean air
- Champion trees, natural environment, being able to see this wonderful old growth forest and learn about it
- Chance for pleasant walking
- Clean
- Clean environment, not crowded, nice trails, clean facility
- Clean, well maintained, friendly staff, great information, clean restrooms
- Convenience, quality of park
- Despite really tall trees, we saw quite a few birds
- Displays
- Diversity in the wilderness
- Diversity of forest
- Ease of walking in the woods; we got the experience of being in thick forest with easy walking
- Ease to get around. Small groups of people. Trail markers on trees.
- Easy access, boardwalk, trail hike and film
- Education of youth in old growth, etc.
- Everything
- Exercise, solitude, nature
- Experiencing such a unique place
- Exploring nature while hiking/walking
- Floodplain forest
- Forest, peaceful, beauty
- Free camping, night hiking
- Freedom to explore/walk to observe and enjoy nature
- Friendliness of ranger (Mr. Greeter) and meeting other interesting people. Beautiful weather. Educational.
- Friendly staff
- Friendly staff and volunteers
- Friendly staff and volunteers in visitor center and on walks
- Golden Crowned Kinglet, red-headed woodpecker, birds in general, swamp
- Good condition - all trails are open
- Good experience, staff informative, easy to hike boardwalk

- o Good hiking trails
- o Good kayaking and fee free
- o Good trails, solitude
- o Gorgeous swamp - beautiful day; trees/forests awesome
- o Great bird watching, wonderful talk by volunteer
- o Great park
- o Great ranger-led canoe trip
- o Guided tour
- o Having access, via the boardwalk, to wet areas I would not have been able to see.
- o Helpfulness of staff
- o Hiking and canoeing
- o Hiking the boardwalks
- o Hiking trails and large trees
- o Hiking was most enjoyable, very quiet
- o Hiking, friendly staff, camping, floodplain forest, visitor center bathroom
- o I like hiking and photography
- o I liked the inside. It was well done. I also liked the boardwalk.
- o I only had about 40 minutes and I loved the boardwalk trail in the beautiful trees
- o Immersion in nature
- o Information from staff, visitor center exhibits, and movie
- o Interesting, great boardwalk hike
- o It satisfied our wish to see - be in - the swamp, enjoy a nice day
- o It was quiet. Maps were helpful.
- o It was so serene and quiet. Lovely birds and lots of them. Great boardwalks.
- o It was very unexpected
- o It's a fun place to walk
- o It's a peaceful place to hike
- o It's not often one sees the beauty of such a place
- o It's the best place in Columbia
- o Just enjoying being outdoors in such an interesting place
- o Just love the floodplain/swamp
- o Kayaking on Cedar Creek
- o Knowledge shared by the paid and volunteer staff
- o Large trees, clean facility, the politeness of staff
- o Large variety of wildlife, especially off-trail
- o Leadership of John Cely and his knowledge of park and its resources
- o Loblolly pines
- o Long boardwalk through swamp
- o Long, quiet hike, bird calls, champion trees, cypress "knees"
- o Long, well-marked trails
- o Lots of birds
- o Love the trees
- o Natural forest setting, quietness, beautiful
- o Nature, history, trails

- Nature; access to nature via walking trail
- New environment, peace, quiet
- Nice trails, cypress trees, trails well-marked
- Nice walk with self-guided tour, view, learning
- No crowds, boardwalk, ranger
- Old forest, solitude, fresh air
- Old growth trees
- Old growth trees
- Opportunity for fresh air, quiet and exercise - free of charge experience
- Opportunity for good conversation. Learned about woodpeckers and cypress knees.
- Outdoors
- Outside/nature solitude
- Outstanding interactions with staff and amazing resource
- Overnight camping with my son
- Peace and large trees
- Peace and quiet
- Peace and quiet, free camping
- Peace, order, clean
- Peace, paths, preservation of trees and landscape and personnel
- Peaceful
- Peaceful sounds of nature during our walk
- Peaceful, beautiful walk
- Peaceful, very few visitors, pleasant weather, no mosquitos
- Peaceful, well-maintained, but rural trails for running
- Peacefulness and beauty of old growth woods
- Peacefulness, the walk, boardwalk, wildlife
- Preservation of swamp
- Quality and quantity of trails
- Quiet and cypress
- Quiet and natural
- Quiet and solitude
- Quiet and solitude of kayaking Cedar Creek. All the birds.
- Quiet getaway, nature
- Quiet walk to stretch legs
- Quiet, beauty
- Quiet, beauty, friendly staff
- Quiet, boardwalk, small number of visitors
- Quiet, condition/length of boardwalk
- Quiet, friendliness and helpfulness of the ranger on duty in the visitor center, numbers on the boardwalk
- Quiet, tree, diversity
- Quiet; Loved the trees
- Ranger was most helpful, knowledgeable and friendly - Kathleen
- Rangers and their ability to communicate their knowledge of park natural history
- Rangers and volunteers were friendly, knowledgeable, and motivated

- Remoteness, quiet
- Scenery
- Scenery
- Scenery within the park, trails
- Scenic views with explanations in brochures. Wildlife, foliage, nature, solitude.
- Scenic walks, history of parks
- Seeing a preserved forest and it was very peaceful
- Seeing the floodplain environment
- Seeing the large trees on our hikes; hikes were well-marked
- Self boardwalk tour and quality of brochure and information at each marked station; mural in visitors center
- Serenity
- Silence
- Solitude
- Solitude
- Solitude
- Solitude
- Solitude
- Solitude
- Solitude, champion trees and hiking on trails
- Solitude and trails for walking and enjoying each other and the area around us
- Solitude of the trails
- Solitude on the trail and seeing some wild pigs
- Solitude on the trails and the option to sign-up for a canoe trip and guided tour
- Solitude, ease of access, minimal expense, helpful/friendly National Park Service personnel
- Solitude, easy walking trails, visitor center
- Solitude, majesty of old growth forest, wildlife
- Solitude, natural balance of nature
- Solitude, nice trails, no mosquitos. Loved idea of canoe trip led - didn't know enough in advance.
- Solitude, plants, animals
- Solitude, quietness, and sounds of nature
- Solitude, silence, excellent trails, well-maintained foot bridges and boardwalks, wild pigs
- Solitude, the forest itself, beautiful camping spot, boardwalk, trails
- Staff
- Staff, boardwalk
- Staff very nice and helpful. Trails well marked and easy to follow. Good directional signs. Maps corresponded to trails and bridges.
- Swamp environment, trees, birds
- That it is a national Park
- That we were here in February and had the park to ourselves. Could be leisurely walking, no bugs at this time of year.
- The abundance of birds - many types
- The amazing trees and the boardwalk
- The bald cypress root structures were something we had never seen before, and they really made the hike

- o   The beauty and peacefulness
- o   The beauty of the old growth floodplain forest and the champion trees, especially the loblolly pines
- o   The beauty of the park
- o   The beauty of the place, the peace and quiet
- o   The big trees, birds singing, squirrels
- o   The birds (Barred Owl) and on a previous visit spiders and dragon flies
- o   The boardwalk trail and pamphlet
- o   The boardwalk trail and the big trees
- o   The boardwalk, different landscape, learning about the ecosystem
- o   The boardwalk; the entire visit was very enjoyable
- o   The boardwalks were fun and well-maintained
- o   The boardwalks were well done
- o   The chance to see a biome we had never seen
- o   The freedom to just go
- o   The great loblolly pines and ancient trees
- o   The hike and guide to read
- o   The hogs were so cool
- o   The kayaking opportunities and knowledgeable staff/volunteers
- o   The magnificence of the old growth forest
- o   The mystery, magic, and majesty of the trees, the boardwalks, the Pileated woodpecker
- o   The natural beauty and solitude and no litter. Cleanest place in the county.
- o   The natural experience
- o   The nature and beauty of the park. I like the turtles; fiance likes the "crazy squirrels."
- o   The old growth forests
- o   The opportunity to enjoy hiking and sightseeing with our dogs
- o   The peace and quiet
- o   The peacefulness of the trails and being able to visit/see one of the last floodplains
- o   The pileated woodpecker
- o   The quiet walk on the boardwalk trail and the interesting scenery
- o   The quiet walks on the trails
- o   The quiet, the swamps, the boardwalk, the staff
- o   The ranger who led our tour was stellar
- o   The relaxing atmosphere, friendly park rangers
- o   The serenity and safety of walking around the trails
- o   The solitude and sounds of nature
- o   The solitude on the trail and the wildlife
- o   The solitude, friendliness of staff
- o   The talks with park rangers
- o   The trails - seeing the native plants and wildlife
- o   The trails were wonderful; well taken care of; loved boy scout bridges
- o   The trees - Wow
- o   The trees and the quiet
- o   The uniqueness of this eco-system
- o   The variety of plants to observe within a 2-hour walk

- The vegetation, especially the trees
- The way the trails (Western Lake Loop) weave through the old growth forest. The condition of the trails was great.
- The whole park
- The wooden path, good condition, friendly staff, film, AV presentation, restrooms, parking
- Touring with a volunteer guide (John Cely) to tell us information about what we were seeing
- Trails
- Trails
- Trails
- Trails and big trees, no mosquitos or humidity
- Trails open and clear for hiking
- Trails to hike
- Trails were well marked and an enjoyable hike
- Trees
- Trees
- Trees
- Trees
- Trees
- Trees and walkways
- Trees, boardwalk
- Trees, great trails, quiet
- Trees, knees in the water
- Trees, trails
- Twenty-one points of interest along the boardwalk trail
- Uncrowded, pleasant
- Undisturbed wilderness, quiet, bird life
- Unique forest, boardwalk, very pleasant staff and volunteers, John
- Unique park, boardwalks well-maintained, wonderful interaction (conversing with rangers)
- Unique primeval-like old-growth floodplain forest setting, which is beautiful and serene
- Unique swamp forest, no bugs, zero on mosquito meter
- Very free-form exploration
- Very good boardwalk trails. The marked places of interest. Seeing the large bald cypress trees.
- Very peaceful
- Viewing the forest and birds from boardwalk, talking with staff and volunteers
- Visited in February; unfortunately, not much blooming and little animal activity, but no mosquitos
- Visitor center was very helpful
- Walk
- Walking
- Walking in an old growth forest
- Walking in quiet woods with knowledgeable ranger and volunteer
- Walking in woods, seeing big trees
- Walking on the elevated boardwalk trail
- Walking the elevated boardwalk
- Walking Weston Lake Loop
- We enjoyed hiking the boardwalk and completing the Junior Ranger program with the kids

- We enjoyed seeing the beautiful old growth forest and the large trees
- We experienced the vast boardwalk and enjoyed it
- We had a beautiful day and we loved the trails, the champion trees
- We like being alone to hear, see, audio record and photograph nature
- We love nature. The boardwalk was awesome.
- We love the trails, the quiet. A wonderful place to hike. It was my birthday.
- We were unfamiliar with this type of swamp - very beautiful
- Weather, boardwalk
- Well-designed boardwalk showed key features of the park
- Well-kept trails, Junior Ranger program
- Well-kept, nice trails
- Wilderness
- Woodpeckers

Q32b. What did you and your personal group like least about your visit to Congaree NP?

- Airplane noise
- Airplane noise
- All good
- Almost no parking
- Any sign of man, ie: Solo cups discarded alongside boardwalks
- Bald Cypress trees
- Barking dogs
- Boardwalk was made of wood. Thought that was a bit weird to have in a national park.
- Boy scouts a bit rowdy
- Came before blooming season
- Campgrounds need upgrading. Need to have water at after hours campground. Need sanitation facilities at Bluff Campground.
- Can't think of anything remotely negative
- Chilly wind
- Could you move it to my backyard? Nothing - it was a beautiful visit, perfect weather.
- Couldn't stay longer
- Crying babies
- Cut our hike short because we thought gate locked at 5. It doesn't.
- Dearth of wildlife (in Feb)
- Destruction by wild pigs. Unexpected water on Oakridge Trail.
- Destructive signs of pigs
- Did not have enough time - not your fault
- Did not have enough time to spend
- Did not see hogs
- Didn't have time to take a longer hike
- Didn't see as many birds as I'd hoped for
- Didn't understand which trails we could take a dog on
- Difficult to rate progress on unmarked trails
- Distance from home - 30 miles. If closer, we would come about once a week.
- Distance from major roads
- Dogs on boardwalk
- Dogs on boardwalk and trails. Most trails start and end on boardwalk.
- Enjoying the quiet and peace
- Everything was great
- Evidence of destruction by pigs everywhere
- Exceeded expectations
- Feral pigs - get rid of them
- Few signs to help you find it
- Fewer animal sightings - wrong time of year
- Filling out this extremely long form
- Forgot to bring water
- Getting to the bluff site too late to get a fire ring
- Got conflicting information from rangers and volunteers

- Great experience - no negatives
- Having to leave my dog in the car for much of our hike, but I understand why
- Hearing gunshots
- Honestly, pretty boring
- How clean and maintained
- Hurricane Hugo trees - dead
- I can't think of any issues, I had a limited 2.5 hr. visit. Perhaps the signage to get into/to the park
- I didn't expect to hear airplanes, but it didn't really affect the experience
- I wanted more information about wildlife while on trails. Had to identify via iPhone.
- I would like to see a few benches on the trails
- Inability to use boardwalk because dogs not allowed - feel missed best viewing
- Inefficiency of check-in after hike. We were exhausted, but had to wait due to only one clipboard with eight forms on it. Should have been one form per clipboard.
- It rained during my visit
- It was all good
- It was near impossible to find a clear bank to fish the Congaree River
- It was only great. To think I had no idea it existed only one week ago.
- It was raining
- Lack of campsites for tenting
- Lack of canoe tours, maybe allow some canoe times for people on a first-come-first-served basis
- Lack of deadwood
- Lack of detailed information and education. Too broad, not enough scientific detail.
- Lack of lodging in the park
- Lack of markers identifying plant life and trees. Not numbers, actually tell us what we see.
- Lack of parking, very overzealous law enforcement on power trips
- Lack of signs for campground - after hours parking not a good description
- Last year we planned a visit and had reserved a spot on the ranger-led canoe trip. We had to cancel that trip and were disappointed to learn that the canoe trips have been cut way back.
- Liked all of it
- Liked it all
- Liked it all
- Liked it all
- Litter
- Long walk from car to #5 campsite
- Loud children
- Loud people who scared away birds
- Loud talking visitors
- Loud, running children on boardwalk
- Loved everything
- Loved everything
- Marginal to poor water quality. The Congaree River seems to be in pretty bad shape.
- Maybe that there was nothing to eat nearby
- More trails
- Mosquitos
- Mosquitos

- My feet hurt
- Need more rangers
- Needed a bathroom halfway around boardwalk
- Needed a bit more marking and directions on paths
- No animals
- No opportunity to go out in a boat unless you canoed
- No plaques stating the age of the trees and the boardwalk was too long
- No ranger-led offered, improve signage
- No restrooms or water at campground
- No signage explaining the area, trees, etc.
- No water available in organized camping area
- Noise - airplane, train
- Noise - trains, airplanes
- Noise of jets
- None
- None
- None
- Not allowed to walk our dogs on boardwalk
- Not being able to kayak or canoe
- Not being able to take dog on boardwalks, long way around to trails
- Not enough informational markers along the boardwalk
- Not enough time
- Not enough trails, especially in the eastern half of the park
- Not having the boardwalks better marked
- Not much there, or at least minimal variety
- Not really a dislike, but with our last minute trip to South Carolina, we were too late (and disappointed) to be unable to go on ranger-led canoe trip
- Not very good road signage on highways leading to the park
- Nothing
- Nothing
- Nothing
- Nothing
- Nothing
- Nothing
- Nothing
- Nothing
- Nothing
- Nothing
- Nothing
- Nothing
- Nothing
- Nothing
- Nothing
- Nothing
- Nothing

- o   Nothing
- o   Nothing
- o   Nothing - wonderful respite
- o   Nothing noted - it was a positive experience
- o   Nothing specific
- o   Nothing, except maybe mosquitos
- o   Only one backcountry camping site
- o   Other people's litter (beer cans) on the beach at the river
- o   Our dog couldn't come on all of the trails that we wanted to go on
- o   Parking was tight - not enough spaces
- o   People on trails
- o   People who had their dogs and bikes on the boardwalk
- o   Pigs in the backcountry
- o   Poor sign from main road
- o   Primitive camping - no bath house at campground
- o   Proximity to noise, no water source at Bluff Campground
- o   Railings on low boardwalk broken
- o   Rain
- o   Rain
- o   Rain during our visit
- o   Rainy day, but you cannot control that
- o   Rainy weather. I know you need it, but...
- o   Roads leading to it creeped me out
- o   Sameness of the forest - homogeneity
- o   Saw less wildlife than we expected. Not a lot to see if you don't do a lot of hiking.
- o   Seeing the damage from wild pigs
- o   Seeing the littler in the creek, but we picked up what we could
- o   Seeing trash - offer incentive for collected trash
- o   Signs going to park
- o   Some guys had built a fire in the backcountry and did not put it out
- o   Some maintenance needed on trails. Benches would be good.
- o   Special trees
- o   Strange man on trail
- o   Surrounding area
- o   Survey questions upon arrival in visitor center
- o   Tall dead trees along boardwalk
- o   Teenagers swinging on trees during last visit
- o   That canoe tour wasn't available that day
- o   That we didn't plan more time there
- o   That we only had a few hours - would have liked more time there
- o   The brevity of the visit
- o   The cold weather
- o   The crazy-ass spider that tried eating my fiancé's head, and it looked like there was oil in the water
- o   The difficulty in reserving ranger-guided canoe tours

- The evidence of wild pigs, i.e., tearing up the ground
- The outhouses at the campground are falling apart; the floor is rotting; no showers or running water
- The trail brochure was a little confusing
- The trail map was confusing
- There is nothing even close to outside of the park - restaurants and activities
- There was no bad experience
- There was no scenic outlook, but that's no fault of the park, as it is a swamp
- There was only one trail that allowed bikes and it was only one mile long
- There was some confusion at the major trail intersections where the Weston Lake Loop Trail continued
- This survey
- Thunder and rain
- Tires were slashed at river take out and van was towed
- Too few opportunities to sign up for special events - volume limitations, canoe trips
- Too hot
- Trail signage - need more information on signs about distances, should use map boards
- Trails could use more signage
- Trash on sand bank on the Congaree River on the river trail
- Unexpected cool weather
- Unless we missed the exhibit in the VC, there's no stand alone exhibit about the bald cypress roots. We did find the one panel in the pine "forest" about the tree
- Very difficult to find and no other signs to guide you into the park
- Visited in February; unfortunately, not much blooming and little animal activity, but no mosquitos
- Was not unhappy with visit
- We are coming back. Love it.
- We asked about an event schedule. The staff said there are none.
- We did not experience anything negative
- We enjoyed all aspects of the park
- We enjoyed it all
- We enjoyed ourselves that day just as we always do. Nothing negative to say.
- We got there too late and would have liked to have spent more time
- We saw trash underneath boardwalk and people ignoring the 'no dogs' sign and bringing their dogs on trails
- We should have come when leaves on trees formed full canopy
- We were unable to attend the owl prowl. Would it be possible to have an owl hospital? Or video?
- Weston Lake Loop Trail could use more guideposts or benches. I realize the swamp may not allow this.
- Wished we could have rented a canoe on the weekday

Q33. Congaree NP was established because of its significance to the nation. In your opinion, what is the national significance of this park?

- A preserved old growth floodplain
- A unique biological environment
- A very rare wilderness
- Ability to handle flooding and naturally purifying water. Historic trees.
- Ability to see virgin forest
- All national parks are extremely important
- All parks are significant
- An example of floodplain and forest
- An untouched swath of land that serves as a biodiversity haven and an original reference point
- Ancient forest, floodplain
- Appreciating swamp
- As a unique eco-system found nowhere else
- As one of the few remaining old growth floodplain forests, the preservation of this park is vital for historical, educational, and natural reasons
- Awesome
- Big trees, biodiversity, saving old growth forest
- Bioreserve
- Biodiversity safe haven for wild animals, old trees, climate control
- Biological diversity combined with accessibility
- Biosphere, temperate forest
- Bottomland hardwood
- Breeding and habitat for unique and at risk wildlife
- Champion trees saved from loggers, birds
- Champion trees, old bottomland hardwood forest
- Champion trees, wildlife diversity, wilderness preservation
- Champion/large trees, floodplains
- Civil War history
- Conservation
- Conservation of our natural habitat
- Cross section of unusual and rare biomes
- Cypress swamps, wildlife, natural heritage
- Cypress trees and other
- Cypress, tupelo trees, large pines
- Don't know
- Don't know
- Ecology and natural resources
- Exemplifies a particularly important type of biosphere
- Exposure to a different ecological setting
- Few such parks on the East coast; largest remaining old growth forest in the east; diversity of wildlife
- Floodplain forest
- Floodplain forest is a unique ecosystem, and it was protected through a grassroots movement
- Floodplain old growth forest

- Floodplain trees
- Floodplains and forest
- Forest (old growth floodplain)
- Forest preservation
- Forest protection, history of area, plants and animals
- Great place to visit nature
- Great significance
- Historical
- History and ecosystem
- History being preserved
- Huge trees
- Huge trees
- I don't know
- I would have to say the large, unique trees and the swamp
- Importance of maintaining our natural heritage, preserving swamp lands, etc.
- Important
- Important
- Important forest, but don't understand its criticality as a national park vs. national preserve, monument, etc.
- Important natural resource
- Interesting forest, worth preserving and protecting from development
- It adds to the overall recreational and scenic choices for all of us
- It has some natural scenes that I have not seen elsewhere
- It helps to preserve history and natural ecosystem
- It is a unique environment, so it must be preserved
- It is a wonderful refuge for wildlife and a possible environmental barometer that should be studied
- It is one of the last old growth forests around. It shows how the land used to be and how detrimental humans can be to the planet.
- It is our "national swamp"
- It is rare
- It preserves a slice of what this area once was like
- It preserves a world that normally would be destroyed by ourselves
- It preserves/protects the largest tract of bottomland hardwood forest
- It shows what our forest can be
- It was an important ecosystem within its borders
- It was one of 3 or 4 on the east coast
- It's a very unique place with the floodplains and old hardwood forest, both which cannot be experience anywhere else
- It's beauty
- It's important
- It's important to conserve these areas for future generations
- Its significance to South Carolina, its habitats
- Its status as old growth floodplain habitat, which is rare and yet critical for water and soil quality, wildlife, etc.
- It's the last remaining section of hardwood old growth southeast bottomlands remaining

o   It's the last stand of old growth pine forest
o   It's unique; tall trees, floodplain, very cool
o   Its biodiversity as well as the historical significance of the area
o   Its history and natural resources
o   Its unique ecosystem
o   Keeping a part of nature alive
o   Large trees
o   Large trees
o   Largest deciduous forest in world
o   Last of old forest
o   Learn about swamp of southern states and tall trees. Protects wilderness area from development so
        all people can enjoy it.
o   Location of park
o   Magnificent and rare old growth forest
o   Maintaining wetland habitats
o   Minimal
o   Monument trees and floodplain
o   Natural habitat
o   Natural habitat
o   Natural habitat and preservation
o   Natural history of unmatched character
o   Natural South Carolina landscape, old growth canopy
o   Natural, wild part of our state. Old growth pines and habitat need to be preserved.
o   Nature is being saved
o   Nature, swamp, trees and their knees
o   No other park like it
o   Not sure
o   Not sure why this qualifies as a NP - does not compare to most other NP's
o   Offers a myriad of opportunities; great place to visit
o   Old forest natural resource reserve, quiet and designated trails, accessibility to old growth plain forest
o   Old growth
o   Old growth cypress
o   Old growth ecosystem
o   Old growth floodplain forest
o   Old growth floodplain, biodiversity
o   Old growth forest
o   Old growth forest
o   Old growth forest
o   Old growth forest
o   Old growth forest
o   Old growth forest and public facility
o   Old growth forest and swamp
o   Old growth forest and wildlife preserve
o   Old growth forest on a floodplain basin
o   Old growth forest preservation

- o Old growth forest that has been preserved
- o Old growth forest, big trees, biodiversity
- o Old growth forest/habitat
- o Old growth habitat for unique plants and animals
- o Old growth pine indicative wilderness
- o Old growth tree preservation
- o Old growth trees
- o Old growth trees
- o Old growth trees, unique natural beauty
- o Old growth, conservation
- o Old growth, natural setting
- o Oldest old growth forest
- o Oldest old growth forest. Never seen anything like it, just moved here.
- o One of a kind
- o One of last stands of old growth floodplain forest. Ecosystem, size of them.
- o One of the few remaining old growth forests in the world
- o One-of-a-kind
- o Only one of its kind in North America. So rich in its history and beauty.
- o Preservation
- o Preservation
- o Preservation of a significant environment
- o Preservation of animal and plant life, especially the wild pigs
- o Preservation of floodplain environment, trees, birds
- o Preservation of natural areas
- o Preservation of nature and a place to go that doesn't cost an arm and leg
- o Preservation of old growth floodplain forest
- o Preservation of old growth floodplain forest
- o Preservation of old growth floodplain forest and its accessibility
- o Preservation of old growth forest. National park available in South Carolina.
- o Preservation of the highest deciduous forest canopy on earth
- o Preservation of unique species
- o Preserve for future generations
- o Preserve natural history of old growth floodplain forest
- o Preserve old growth
- o Preserve the swamp and old growth timber for future generations
- o Preserved old growth forest with champion trees
- o Preserves first growth forest
- o Preserving a largely vanished ecosystem
- o Preserving a rare environment
- o Preserving habitat for plants and animals, allowing people to experience this preservation
- o Preserving nature
- o Preserving plants and ecosystems
- o Preserving resources
- o Preserving tall trees and introducing people to importance of ecosystem

- o   Preserving the natural habitat of the old growth floodplain
- o   Preserving this wonderful, unique area for future generations
- o   Preserving unique ecosystem
- o   Preserving what is left of this dramatic ecosystem and letting Americans enjoy it without impacting it too much
- o   Preserving wilderness
- o   Preserving wilderness areas and our natural resources
- o   Priceless
- o   Probably very little...things change, neither for better nor for worse, oftentimes
- o   Protect old growth plants and species. Preserve floodplain for regional security.
- o   Protect trees and wildlife. Have a place to study.
- o   Protected for the future
- o   Protecting an ecosystem that would be destroyed in the absence of the park
- o   Protecting the past/future
- o   Protecting wild lands and diverse species
- o   Protection and preservation of unique wilderness area
- o   Protection of beautiful spaces
- o   Protection of old forest floodplain
- o   Protection of old growth forest and research opportunities
- o   Protects an ecosystem that would have been destroyed by development
- o   Rarity of old growth forest, birds
- o   Rarity of species
- o   Record trees, massive land area preserved
- o   Recreation, restore nature
- o   Remnant bottomland forest
- o   Sample of what once was a larger forest - lowland swamp
- o   Saving a piece of virgin South Carolina for future generations to see
- o   Saving an old growth floodplain forest from destruction and helping people understand its significance
- o   Saving old growth trees and maintaining habitat for native plants and animals
- o   Saving one of the last virgin forests in the eastern USA
- o   See a real forest - nature at its best
- o   Seeing what nature was like before man intruded
- o   Show that SC has a history to be explored
- o   Showing people why it is important to pay attention to nature
- o   Size of the forest
- o   Size, location, trails
- o   So unique
- o   Special ecosystem and habitat, plant and wildlife
- o   Swamp and its history. Trees - bald cypress, loblolly, etc.
- o   Swamp ecosystem
- o   Swampland trees
- o   Swamps are part of nature. Our parks are more than big trees and waterfalls. Swamps are unique ecosystems.
- o   Tall loblolly pines, wetlands, mangroves
- o   That our nation is supportive of parks and preserving natural habitats

- That part of our country's natural beauty has been preserved in its undisturbed state for citizens to experience now and in the future. This is a wonderful gift.
- The beautiful creation God made left untouched
- The beauty of an old growth forest
- The biosphere and where/how it fits into the overall ecology
- The champion trees and the collection of old growth trees
- The fact that it is an old growth bottomland forest
- The fact that it is one of the few remaining old growth floodplain forests in the US
- The heritage to the area
- The history
- The importance of protecting wetlands
- The importance of tree conservation because of animal dependence on trees, especially woodpeckers
- The largest remaining old-growth bottomland forest
- The old growth forest
- The old growth forest in a southern setting that is easily accessible in many different ways
- The old growth trees
- The old growth trees and the floodplain
- The only old growth floodplain - nothing else like it
- The park is the remains of a very productive ecosystem
- The preservation of its unique environs
- The preservation of the large bald cypress trees
- The preservation of this beautiful and rare landscape and ecosystem
- The rarity of old growth forests. Also, the total quiet. An ideal swamp.
- The swamp and trees
- The swamp areas and trees, wildlife. A place for quiet exploration and beauty.
- The swamp, the cypress trees and knees, the old growth, etc.
- The tallest deciduous canopy, maybe in the world. The biodiversity.
- The trees
- The trees and the protection of the floodplain
- The trees, the access - easy, but not invasive or intrusive
- The unique terrain and habitat makes this a unique national treasure worth preserving
- The unusualness of the trees
- The wildlife and the trees that it protects
- There is no other place quite like it and it should be preserved for future generations
- To be able to imagine what it was like when it was first explored
- To maintain a unique environment for current and future generations
- To preserve natural resources and wildlife and access to public
- To preserve old forest
- To preserve the old growth floodplain forest
- To preserve the old growth trees, etc. The citizen's role in saving the special space, the activism.
- To preserve this chunk of nature - a special place
- To preserve this piece of nature in its pristine condition
- Tranquil environment close to a state capitol
- Tree protection

- o Tree species
- o Trees
- o Trees and plants
- o Trees cannot be harvested and nature can take its course
- o Trees, birds
- o Tremendous value to our nation because of the variety and type of plants/wildlife
- o Undisturbed old growth forest
- o Unique landscape, "walk back in time"
- o Unique lowland forest
- o Unique natural environment as surviving old growth coastal forest
- o Unique wilderness preservation
- o Uniqueness of plant specifics
- o Unobstructed by human impact
- o Untouched natural habitat; last forest of its kind, beautiful
- o Untouched nature
- o Untouched resources
- o Very few left that exhibit this untouched environment and old growth forests
- o Very high
- o Very important
- o Very important because we have almost no old growth trees and forests left
- o Very important never to lose
- o Very neat ecosystem
- o Very old trees and wilderness
- o Very significant
- o Very significant
- o Very tall trees, unique landscape, but perhaps not as unique as some. Definitely for the region.
- o We need to preserve old growth forests so kids can see what it was like
- o Wetland environment, cypress knees
- o Wetlands, habitats
- o Where to start - nature is disappearing, must save as much as possible. Important to see how America looked at one time.
- o Wilderness area that needs to be preserved
- o Wilderness area, old growth
- o Wilderness swamp

Q34. If you were a manager planning for the future of Congaree NP, what would you and your personal group propose?

o   A designated area to select camping spots - spread apart in a wilderness area
o   A fee to enter the park
o   A little more promotion - I don't think people know about this park
o   A nice restaurant would be lovely
o   A reminder to take water with you while touring
o   A sign at the beach asking folks to 'carry out' or a trash bin
o   Ability to canoe/kayak during week
o   Acquire more land, especially on west bank
o   Acquiring more land, adding an RV campground
o   Add more about importance of wetlands as earth's filter. Improve/add trail direction signs/maps.
o   Add more staff, ie., rangers and volunteers
o   Add running water at the camping areas
o   Add to boardwalk trail
o   Additional trails
o   Additional trails, Riverside Beach on river trails
o   All photos in the exhibit should identify who took them, date taken, who are the subjects; more
       informational markers explaining flora, fauna and geologic or ground formations in more detail
o   An inn would be nice. Please mark biggest trees better on maps or near trees.
o   An observation tower or canopy walk to get up into the trees
o   Another ranger or two to facilitate canoe program and presentations
o   Ask the military to not fly over the park and involve the local community in the preservation of the park
o   Attempt to hire locals to ensure more long-range success of park/local interactions
o   Balance preservation and use
o   Better camping facility; coordinating with lower Richland
o   Better facilities/area for non-tent campers, RV/trailers aren't given space/picnic table/fire pit
o   Better sign/directions to the park
o   Better signage
o   Better signs of the trails. I did not bring a map of the trails and wanted to get off the boardwalk, but
       wasn't sure of the trail.
o   Better website - no information on picnic area. Educate the public of the value.
o   Bike trail, night hiking guided
o   Boardwalk maintenance
o   Boat tours of 1-2 hour narrated by a ranger or knowledgeable guide
o   Build a 'green' lodge
o   Build a more informative website with research results. Have more programs.
o   Build specified bike paths
o   Build up the area/community surrounding park. "Clean it up"
o   Campground expansion
o   Can't think of anything
o   Cannot think of anything
o   Canopy tour
o   Change to National Monument and use NP resources elsewhere

- Charge a fee for guided kayak tours and increasing the number of tours
- Closer access from car to put kayaks in
- Congaree needs its own sticker for the passport books; it is a hidden treasure. More advertising to let people know about it.
- Continue
- Continue "wilderness" aspect and exotic species work
- Continue natural preservation
- Continue to expand its boundaries. We have enough commercial space and homes. Protect this special place for my grandkids.
- Continue to preserve this wonderful piece of America for our children and grandchildren
- Continue to protect forest, guided tours help educate us to its importance and benefits
- Continue to protect park and watershed as much as possible
- Continued excellent maintenance
- Decent campgrounds, but without cutting any of that wonderful forest. Also, get wealthy people to help acquire more land.
- Do nothing. Leave it alone. Beautiful just the way it is.
- Do what you are doing
- Don't know
- Don't know
- Don't know
- Easy access to an unobstructed canoe trails
- Educate and protect
- Educating the public to the importance of protecting and preserving this natural resource
- Education on importance of old growth forest/biodiversity
- Educational lectures
- Encourage or make mandatory for schools to visit the park
- Encourage outreach and education on native flora and fauna - workshops at local schools
- Enjoyment
- Enlarge the lookout area for viewing the lake. Something about larger bodies of water that fascinate people. Tranquil, serene.
- Everything was perfect
- Expand boundaries and/or emphasize negative impact of litter
- Expand land holdings. Kill wild pigs. Eliminate or control exotics.
- Expand the boardwalk
- Expand the park
- Expand to surrounding countryside to show change in habitat, etc.
- Expanded educational opportunities, increased signage on trails giving specifics on trails
- Expansion, coordination with other nearby preserves, protection from South Carolina highway development
- Family camping
- Fitness, stress reduction
- Further boardwalk trails
- Further promotion of education about the biological and historical significance of the park
- Further wildlife emphasis. Perhaps greater access to trails? But, perhaps not.
- Get involved; participate in group activities

- Get rid of McEntire
- Get ride of the pigs, would like to know more about the different plant communities, how to help in preserving and restoring park to original wildness
- Great just as is
- Guided tours for photographers
- Guided walks off of the boardwalks
- Have only visited one time and had a good experience
- Have program in surrounding towns especially Columbia
- Higher bridges crossing to avoid submersion as often in some trail locations, continued trail maintenance, number and types of programs visitors would enjoy
- Hire more rangers
- I am not a manager
- I would be searching for a way to eliminate the wild pigs or significantly reduce their numbers. They are horribly destructive.
- I would propose mountain bike specific trails. The park would be a great experience on a bike.
- I would purchase as much of the surrounding property as possible
- I would try to preserve as much and for as long as possible. We are too much of a disposable society.
- I'm not sure what takes place already, perhaps triathlons, a fishing tournament on the Congaree with big names, engage local business and people, a music festival, photo competition, harvest specimen trees when they fall, charge fees. Have a storm plan - often trees fall in a big storm; I know that is part of the ecosystem, but something limited, a bird watching event(s), a large group campsite
- Increase signage for direction. Large signs on interstate alerting potential visitors.
- Increase the number of days that the kayak trips are offered
- Increase types of usage to maximize support for national parks
- Increased area so greater preservation area, better access from 601
- Interactive trail map online/web - attracts hikers. Google New Zealand national parks for examples.
- Just getting the word out and having lots of recreation opportunities, like the canoe tours
- Keep funding strong. Make paths clear.
- Keep it as it is
- Keep it as natural as possible
- Keep it just as it is
- Keep it like it is
- Keep it like it is
- Keep it like it is except add boardwalks
- Keep it the same
- Keep more parts primitive, walking trails but not asphalt
- Keep public informed and involved. Do not over develop.
- Keep the park just like it is
- Keep up good job of balancing needs of visitors while protecting park
- Keep up the good work
- Keep up the good work, have knowledgeable people on hand
- Keep visitors to the trails and keep nature as untouched as possible
- Keeping it as natural as possible
- Leave as is

- Leave as is and add more canoe trips
- Limit number of people per day access. More bicycle opportunities if not impacting.
- Limited access to wilderness areas
- Listing miles on directional path signs
- Local outreach. Let the people of Columbia know you are here. Though, I'd prefer to keep Congaree National Park a secret.
- Look for ways to continue to preserve this small, precious piece of nature for future generations to come
- Maintain present quality
- Maintain the path that it's on; keep the area minimalist
- Maintenance, expand borders
- Make it bigger
- Make sure there are small activities throughout the trails to see how the park came about
- Marketing, add a nearby cell tower so visitors can share their experiences via smart phones/social media. Would like to have posted to my Facebook page.
- More "live" data and reports on website - water levels/quality, mosquito report, park conditions/updates
- More access to backcountry
- More activities - ranger-led hikes - and more interactive stuff/information on the boardwalk - mostly. Don't damage much, protect and preserve the natural environment.
- More advertisement
- More advertising and more places to stay around the park area
- More advertising of available programs
- More animals
- More boardwalk
- More boardwalks
- More canoeing
- More exposure to attract more visitors. Better signage.
- More exposure to traveling tourists
- More fishing areas, more trails, more camping areas
- More history of the native people in the area through time, more history of how the park was established
- More information about canoeing and plan of attack for the pigs problem
- More information about the trees and plants on signs or plaques
- More information about the trees, plants, area - make a video. More signage. Update website - correct directions.
- More informative placards/trail brochures for self-guided touring/audio tours
- More interpretation of past human use and impact on park area. Better explanation of "cultural resources" of park area.
- More kayaking opportunities with ranger
- More marketing to public for awareness and for attracting more volunteers, especially seniors
- More participation/outreach in greater Columbia community
- More programs for visitors
- More protection
- More public relations and advertising to get the word out about the park
- More publicity nationally

- More ranger-led canoe trips
- More ranger-led hikes, tours, activities just like this one. More publicity - maybe TV spots.
- More running paths
- More signage; explanation of plant and animal life
- More signs on I95 - advertise
- More staff on weekends
- More trails - interpretive signs along the boardwalk
- More trails - just more trails and the ability to rent kayaks/canoes inside the park
- More trails/accessibility
- More trash receptacles along the trails. More advertising for activities.
- Nature study
- New movie
- No comment
- Not qualified - you all are doing a good job
- Not sure
- Not sure - it's a great park
- Nothing
- Offer kayak and canoe rentals with easy pick-up and drop-off right at the park or very close by
- Old growth forest
- One or two more long trails
- Organized activities
- Permanent overnight accommodations, such as a few cabins, maybe seasonably available
- Placing name plates on or near various trees along boardwalk
- Preservation of the land and expansion of hiking and canoe opportunities
- Preserve and education
- Protect it
- Protect the recreational opportunities while also protecting the resources; educate more about resources; get the state to improve the roads leading to the park
- Provide more access into the park and more trails
- Publicize educational opportunities in SC media
- Put distances on trail signs, ie. fishing trail = X miles
- Ranger out and about answering questions, maybe some visuals as well
- Remove invasive, non-native species - both plant and animal
- RV camping
- Same, picnic and walk
- Satisfied
- Sell some food at visitor center, along with drinks. Update the video.
- Shorter surveys
- Talks about proper hiking and trail care, first-hand educational opportunities
- Tell all visitors of guided tours at visitor center face-to-face
- Thanks for adding to the size of the park; consider a new trail deeper into the park
- The movie was great, only too short for me. How about a longer movie, also? Give people a choice.
- The park is great the way it is. Maybe some picnic tables along the trails.
- To continue to preserve it for many generations to come
- To expand the trails into the east and add another entrance

- To get funding to keep the ATBI protest going
- To highlight more of the history of this area year-round. We enjoyed Congaree Campfire Chronicles.
- To let dogs on the boardwalk. New maps in color that are clearer.
- To maintain it as it is
- To preserve the park from dangers
- To publicize the park to area schools and children's groups and expand the educational programs offered
- To stress the importance of habitat conservation for the survival of plants and animals
- Trails on new areas
- Tree identification signs posted on/near trees to help identify
- Try and expand the park to include river and more floodplains
- Try to balance access to public with peace and tranquility
- Try to limit plane/train noise
- Unsure, everything was fantastic
- Upgrade campgrounds - water at after hours campground, sanitary facilities at Bluff. Expand the trail system. There's only about 2 days worth of hiking there at Congaree National Park.
- Upgrade signage directing attention to specific areas and items of interest
- Upgrade the upper boardwalk. The lower boardwalk is smoother.
- Walk your dog day
- Whatever is necessary to protect this place
- Wood duck boxes
- You need signs at all entrances/trails to entrances stating no dogs on the boardwalk. North from Wise Lake a sign says "1.2 miles to visitor center" and says nothing about the boardwalk.
- Your staff is amazing. Hire more like them.
- Youth programs to get children interested in preserving natural resources

Q35. Is there anything else you and your personal group would like to tell us about your visit to Congaree NP?

o
o   A hidden treasure that is worth the detour
o   All was great
o   Also, arrange for canoe/kayak rentals at the park. I could not locate a guide. Operate more ranger-led canoe trips. Arrange for a guide service to be available right at the park. I wished I could have paddled.
o   Always a pleasure to visit, building family memories
o   Always enjoy it
o   Always love this park
o   Amazing place. Good job.
o   Appreciated reading in state paper about upcoming events there
o   Appreciated the enthusiasm of the staff and volunteers
o   Bathrooms should be open 24 hours a day, or have another available clean option
o   Beautiful place, love to bring family and friends there
o   Better information about gate closure vs. visitor center hours
o   Boardwalks and trails promote access to park areas that would be inaccessible otherwise
o   Campsites looked awesome; we'll stay there instead of in town next time
o   Clear trails - very good with excellent blaze markings
o   Confirmed the greatness of national park system
o   Congaree is a special place and totally amazed my Welsh naturalist friend
o   Do not understand why it's one of 59 national parks vs. other national protected area
o   Enjoyed
o   Enjoyed
o   Enjoyed it
o   Enjoyed it
o   Enjoyed our visit and plan to return
o   Enjoyed our visit. This is too long.
o   Excellent staff
o   Fantastic trails, well marked. Will return.
o   February - perfect time to visit. Love the mosquito meter. And dog trail.
o   Good trip
o   Got several lifers
o   Great experience
o   Great place
o   Great visit; park staff was exceptionally helpful; love the skeeter meter
o   Had a great time
o   Had a great time and no bugs
o   Had fun on a beautiful winter day
o   Helpful and friendly staff
o   I am excited about signing up for a canoe trip
o   I enjoyed it. Boardwalk needs the mileage on map and have smaller walk.
o   I frequent national parks. I love the purpose. Keep up good work.
o   I had a good time

- I like the fact that most of the park is undeveloped; I'd like more trails, a larger main visitor center with more exhibits, but I wouldn't want any roads through the park or a 2nd visitor center
- I really enjoyed the Friday mid-day tech talks by experts in November-December 2011
- I took a group of Benedict College students today. Several of my students said they had never been to a national park before.
- I was extremely impressed by the board walk and the natural trails
- I'll be back
- I'm glad that this is a national park and just 2 hour drive from my home
- Interesting and unique. Easy to find.
- Interpretive staff was excellent. Law enforcement was unprofessional and of little help. They work for us.
- It has been a marvelous visit
- It is a peaceful and harmonious place to visit
- It was a great experience on a lovely day, helped by the friendliness of the ranger on duty
- It was a great experience. We really loved the mosquito dial.
- It was a lot of fun. Thanks.
- It was a nice walk; we enjoyed spending time with our loved one in a serene safe environment
- It was a wonderful surprise and valuable walking tour
- It was excellent
- It was great
- It was great
- It was great
- It was nice. Thank you.
- It was wonderful. Thanks to all who preserved it and made it possible.
- It was wonderful. We will return often.
- It's a great opportunity to build family memories. Thank you.
- It's hard to improve upon
- Joe (volunteer) and young female national park employee were very helpful
- Just a pleasant surprise and a place of beauty
- Keep up the good work
- Keep up the good work
- Leave it alone. It is very beautiful.
- Loved it. We will be back.
- Loved the park overall - thank you
- Loved the park. Our ranger was great. Loved the owl prowl. Personnel at desk were extremely helpful.
- Lovely facility, enjoyed video, enthusiastic rangers and volunteers
- Lovely park - Thank you to all staff (super)
- Miriam was less than knowledgeable compared to other rangers we have experienced. Increase her preparation so she can confidently answer basic questions.
- More advertising in southeast region
- More rewarding and interesting than anticipated. Thank you for all your work.
- Movie/film not informative enough - birds, trees names
- My visit was short and spontaneous (a road trip); it is a gem of a park, I had never heard of it but saw it on a map - perhaps more advertising. I will plan to visit again when I have more time.
- Nice experience

- o Park is litter free. Ranger was pleasant. Thank you.
- o Park rangers Kate and Corinne were especially helpful/knowledgeable with information on the park
- o Passport stamp collectors - old stamp Congaree Swamp National Memorial - retired?
- o Place boardwalk maps in more visible and accessible location right at beginning of boardwalk. Several visitors I met on boardwalk asked where I'd found the boardwalk map. They walked past the box on side of building.
- o Please give better information about photographs used in interpretive exhibits in visitor center - date taken at a minimum, but name of photographer if know, names of subjects if known
- o Please identify dates and photographers on pictures on display in visitor center
- o Please include mileage information on trail signs
- o Positive
- o Proofread trail guide - 'Saturday' is not spelled correctly
- o Quite an enjoyable visit
- o Ranger greeter was very informative
- o Ranger Kathleen is a rock star
- o Ranger O'Brien was delightful
- o Rangers and volunteers need to work on their interpersonal skills and educating volunteers on camping permits
- o Rangers David and Terry stopped and volunteered to take our picture together. Ranger in the visitor center gave us a tutorial on owls because we were disappointed that we could not attend owl prowl.
- o Really enjoyed the experience - wonderful. Had never seen B. cypress, etc. Saw hooded merganser for the 1st time and pileated woodpecker entertained us for quite awhile.
- o Research is important, but the main emphasis of a national park should be to make it visitor friendly
- o Saw sign on interstate. More exposure of park to public.
- o Some additional context of how the park compares to other federal lands (national forests, national wildlife refuges) in the area
- o South Carolina is very fortunate to have this resource. Thank goodness someone had the foresight to save it.
- o Staff (1) awesome
- o Staff and intern very helpful
- o Staff as visitor center helpful
- o Staff people were very helpful and nice
- o Staff was great, especially Kristin? Corinne?, not sure of ranger's name
- o Staff was great, facilities appropriate for a wild area
- o Staff was very friendly, knowledgeable and helpful; facility nice and park well-maintained
- o Staff were great. It was a wonderful day. Kids loved it.
- o Staff were just lovely, so helpful and positive
- o Staff were really friendly and helpful - enjoyed visited
- o Surprised (delighted) to fine a NP so close to Columbia
- o Survey was too long, too detailed, maybe too difficult for some to follow instructions. Please publish results for visitors.
- o Thank you
- o Thank you all. We all had a wonderful time.
- o Thank you for all that you do and for providing an excellent outdoor experience
- o Thank you for serving America at its parks

- o Thank you for taking care of this place and making it an easy place to walk
- o Thank you for your hard work and keeping the clean restrooms for our family to use. We visit many national parks, state parks, and other outside adventures. Not all places keep the restrooms clean.
- o Thanks
- o Thanks
- o Thanks
- o The boardwalk gets very slick after rain could get dangerous
- o The boardwalk made the walk easy and leaves the landscape undisturbed
- o the information was a little bit scarce regarding plants and animals
- o The National Park Service always does an outstanding job. Thanks.
- o The park staff is excellent. The numerous ranger-led activities are great. I expect I will be visiting at least twice a month. Keep up the good work.
- o The peacefulness was outstanding
- o The ranger and volunteer were quite helpful
- o The ranger was extremely helpful in answering our questions
- o The rangers are a credit to the National Park Service
- o The rangers were fantastic
- o The rangers were so kind and helpful. Thank you.
- o The rangers were very accommodating and knowledgeable
- o The staff and volunteers were super-friendly and answered all my questions with enthusiasm
- o The staff at the visitor center was very helpful; we really enjoyed
- o The staff is exceptional
- o The staff was very nice
- o There should be foreign language brochures available for visitors from other countries
- o There was a lot of loud talking from other visitors. Maybe some 'quiet' signs would help.
- o This park is a jewel. We keep coming back over and over.
- o This sort of place is a spiritual refreshment for my soul. Thanks.
- o Very clean restrooms. Polite staff. Beautiful park.
- o Very friendly and knowledgeable staff and volunteers
- o Very good trip
- o Very helpful rangers and volunteers. Thank you.
- o Very helpful volunteer and paid staff at the visitor center very hospitable
- o Very nice facilities, very very important to keep this area safe from destruction and commercial development
- o Very nice staff - helpful and proud of their park
- o We are coming back to canoe
- o We are so grateful that this incredible place was preserved. Sad that there is so little of it left. Also, the staff was kind enough to let us park in the parking lot overnight because we arrived late. Appreciated not having to fool around late at night.
- o We arrived when it was dark, there were no signs to tell us where the campground was; we didn't know where to turn and once we got to the campground, we thought it was just a trailhead
- o We enjoyed it
- o We had a wonderful day. Rangers friendly and helpful. Benches a help. We will be back.
- o We had a wonderful hike

- We had difficulty finding a park street address for use with GPS. I think you should do some sort of advertising about the "gnomeland" created by the bald cypress roots
- We had lots of fun on the boardwalk trail, but would like more detailed information on the stations 1-22
- We have been here several times and we were pleased to see so many people using the park this time perhaps because it was on a weekend, but it's always been underutilized on earlier visits
- We have enjoyed our repeated visits here over the past 15-20 years
- We love it. Thank you for all you do to make Congaree National Park such a wonderful place to visit.
- We love the park
- We love the swamp
- We love to see the wild pigs
- We loved it
- We loved it
- We loved it; volunteers were wonderful
- We loved the scenery and the quiet
- We thoroughly enjoyed our visit and will return. This is the 2nd time I have filled out this questionnaire. What happened with the 1st one? Thank you for a beautiful park.
- We visited in February, which is a very nice time, weather-wise, for a visit
- We visited in January and there was no activity at all. A tour would have been good. Area around park area unattractive and intimidating.
- We were impressed with the boardwalks, the work involved in them, and their maintenance. What a great job.
- We were taken away by the parks' beauty and tranquility. The female ranger was very knowledgeable.
- We've been coming our whole lives and love the swamp; I would like the literature about paddling to include more information re: best times of year, appropriate water levels, etc.
- What a jewel. We were totally blown away by your awesome park. So different from our beloved Shenandoah National Park. Loved it.
- What a unique place that is so near - never thought SC had it
- Will try to get back sometime
- Will volunteer
- Wonderful day outing. You do need to check the aging boards of elevated boardwalk out to water's edge off of Weston Lake Trail.
- Wonderful visit
- Would have been nice to have distance markers along trails - how far you've walked or how far to end
- Would have liked water pumps at the campsite, but overall wonderful experience. Will come back.
- Yes, dogs right outside visitor center. Dogs should not be allowed outside visitor center or on any boardwalk. Used park's wheelchairs need repairing - one is in bad shape.
- You've done a great job. Keep it up.
- Your visitors' study needs a lot more space for written answers like this. When I agreed to take this survey, I thought I might have some input, but there is no room.
- Your volunteers and rangers are very helpful and knowledgeable

Appendix 1: The Questionnaire

Congaree Nat ona Park V s tor Study
OMB Approva 1024-0224
Exp rat on date: 2011

2

United States Department of the Interior

NATIONAL PARK SERVICE
Congaree Nat ona Park
100 Nat ona Park Road
Hopk ns, SC 29061

IN REPLY REFER TO:

Dear V s tor:

Thank you for part c pat ng n th s mportant study. Our goa s to earn about the expectat ons, op n ons, and nterests of v s tors to Congaree Nat ona Park. Th s nformat on w ass st us n our efforts to better manage th s park and to serve you.

Th s quest onna re s on y be ng g ven to a se ect number of v s tors, so your part c pat on s very mportant! It shou d on y take about 20 m nutes after your v s t to comp ete.

When your v s t s over, p ease comp ete th s quest onna re. Sea t n the postage pa d enve ope prov ded and drop t n any U.S. ma box.

If you have any quest ons, p ease contact Margaret L tt ejohn, NPS VSP D rector, Park Stud es Un t, Co ege of Natura Resources, P.O. Box 441139, Un vers ty of Idaho, Moscow, Idaho 83844-1139, phone: 208-885-7863, ema : tt ej@u daho.edu.

We apprec ate your he p.

S ncere y,

Tracy Swartout
Super ntendent

Social Science Program
National Park Service
U.S. Department of the Interior

Visitor Services Project

Congaree National Park

Visitor Study

3

DIRECTIONS

1) P ease have the se ected nd v dua (at east 16 years o d) comp ete th s quest onna re.

2) Answer the quest ons carefu y s nce each quest on s d fferent.

3) For quest ons that use c rc es (O), p ease mark your answer by f ng n the c rc e w th b ack or b ue nk. P ease do not use penc .

Like this: Not like this: ⬤ Ⓧ ⊘

4) Sea t n the postage pa d enve ope prov ded.

5) Drop t n a U.S. ma box.

Thank you!

PRIVACY ACT and PAPERWORK REDUCTION ACT statement:

16 U.S.C. 1a-7 author zes co ect on of th s nformat on. Th s nformat on w be used by park managers to better serve the pub c. Response to th s request s vo untary. No act on may be taken aga nst you for refus ng to supp y the nformat on requested. Your name s requested for fo ow-up ma ng purposes on y. When ana ys s of the quest onna re s comp eted, a name and address f es w be destroyed. Thus the permanent data w be anonymous. P ease do not put your name or that of any member of your group on the quest onna re. An agency may not conduct or sponsor, and a person s not requ red to respond to, a co ect on of nformat on un ess t d sp ays a currenty va d OMB contro number.

Burden estimate statement: Pub c report ng burden for th s form s est mated to average 20 m nutes per response. D rect comments regard ng the burden est mate or any other aspect of th s form to Margaret L tt ejohn, NPS V s tor Serv ces Project, Co ege of Natura Resources, Un vers ty of Idaho, P.O. Box 441139, Moscow, ID, 83844-1139; ema : tt ej@u daho.edu.

4

Your Visit To Congaree National Park

NOTE n th s quest onna re your **personal group** s def ned as anyone that you are v s t ng the park w th such as spouse fam y fr ends etc. Th s does not nc ude the arger group that you m ght be trave ng w th such as schoo church scouts or tour group.

1. Pr or to your v s t, how d d you and your persona group obta n nformat on about Congaree Nat ona Park (NP)? P ease mark (●) **all that app y.**

   ○ D d not obta n nformat on pr or to v s t ➔ **Go to question 2**

   ○ Chamber of commerce/v s tors bureau/state we come center

   ○ Congaree NP webs te: www.nps.gov/cong

   ○ Other webs tes — Wh ch one(s)? _____

   ○ Fr ends/re at ves/word of mouth

   ○ H ghway s gns

   ○ Inqu ry to park v a phone, ma or e-ma

   ○ Loca bus nesses (hote s, mote s, restaurants, etc.)

   ○ Maps/brochures

   ○ Newspaper/magaz ne art c es

   ○ Other Nat ona Park Serv ce s tes

   ○ Prev ous v s ts

   ○ Schoo c ass/program

   ○ Soc a med a (such as Facebook, Tw tter, etc.)

   ○ Te ev s on/rad o programs/v deos

   ○ Trave gu des/tour books (such as AAA, etc.)

   ○ Other (P ease spec fy) _____

2. Pr or to your v s t, were you and your persona group aware of programs (ranger- ed wa ks, canoe tr ps, presentat ons, schoo group tours, etc.) offered n Congaree NP?

   ○ Yes   ○ No

8. On this visit, which sites did you and your personal group visit in the Congaree NP **area** (within 1-hour drive of the park)? Please mark (●) **all that apply.**

○ EdVenture   ○ Columbia Metropolitan Airport
○ Lake Murray   ○ Columbia Museum of Art
○ National Advocacy Center   ○ Ft. Jackson Army Training Center
○ Riverbanks Zoo   ○ Harbison State Forest
○ Shaw Air Force Base   ○ The State Capitol
○ South Carolina State Museum   ○ University of South Carolina
○ South Carolina State Parks
○ Other (Please specify) _____

9. a) On this trip, did you and your personal group stay overnight away from your **permanent residence** either inside Congaree NP or within the nearby area (within 1-hour drive of the park)?

○ Yes   ○ No → **Go to Question 10**

b) and c) If YES, how many nights did you and your personal group spend in the following types of accommodations? Please write the number of nights stayed.

b) Number of nights inside park		c) Number of nights outside park within 1-hour drive
n/a	Lodge, hotel, motel, cabin, rented condo/home, or bed & breakfast	_____
_____	RV/trailer camping	_____
_____	Tent camping	_____
_____	Backcountry camping	_____
n/a	Personal seasonal residence	_____
n/a	Residence of friends or relatives	_____
_____	Other accommodations (Please specify below)	_____

Inside park _____   Outside park _____

10. a) On this visit to Congaree NP, did you and your personal group wade/canoe/kayak any park trails?

○ Yes   ○ No → **Go on to Question 11**

---

3. a) In 2003, Congaree Swamp National Monument became Congaree NP. Did this name change have any effect on your decision to visit?

○ Yes   ○ No   ○ Not sure

b) If YES, what effect did it have? Please be specific. _____

4. a) Prior to your visit, were you aware of what congressionally designated wilderness is?

○ Yes   ○ No   ○ Not sure

b) If NO, did you and your personal group learn about congressionally designated wilderness during your visit?

○ Yes   ○ No

5. The National Park Service has a policy to control or remove non-native plants and animals from within park boundaries. Non-native species occupy an area that is not part of their natural, historic range, and often originated from another continent or region. Many of these species are invasive and damage park resources. Were you aware of this policy prior to your visit to Congaree NP?

○ Yes   ○ No   ○ Not sure

6. Would you and your personal group be supportive of the control and removal of non-native species at Congaree NP? Please mark (●) **only one** for each option.

a) Non-native plants   ○ Yes   ○ No   ○ Not sure
b) Non-native animals   ○ Yes   ○ No   ○ Not sure

7. On this trip, what was the **primary** reason that you and your personal group came to the Congaree NP **area** (within 1-hour drive of the park)? Please mark (●) **only one.**

○ Resident of the area (within 1-hour drive of the park) → **Go to Question 8**
○ Visit Congaree NP
○ Visit other attractions in the area
○ Visit friends/relatives in the area
○ Traveling through – unplanned visit
○ Business
○ Other (Please specify) _____

b) On this visit, how long did you and your personal group spend visiting Congaree NP? Please estimate in hours/days as ¼, ½, ¾.

    ___ Number of hours **if less than 24 hours**
- OR -
    ___ Number of days **if 24 hours or more**

14. It is the National Park Service's responsibility to protect Congaree NP natural, scenic, and cultural resources while at the same time providing for public enjoyment. How important is protection of the following resources/attributes in the park to you and your personal group? Please mark (●) **one** answer for each resource/attribute.

Resource/attribute	Not important	Somewhat important	Moderately important	Very important	Extremely important
Clean air (visibility)	○	○	○	○	○
Clean water	○	○	○	○	○
Clear night sky (star gazing)	○	○	○	○	○
Cultural history (photographs/artifacts/oral histories)	○	○	○	○	○
Designated wilderness/backcountry	○	○	○	○	○
Educational opportunities	○	○	○	○	○
Historic buildings/archeological sites	○	○	○	○	○
Native plants	○	○	○	○	○
Native wildlife	○	○	○	○	○
Natural quiet/sounds of nature	○	○	○	○	○
Parking availability	○	○	○	○	○
Recreational opportunities	○	○	○	○	○
Scenic views	○	○	○	○	○
Solitude	○	○	○	○	○

15. a) Prior to this visit were you and your personal group aware that Congaree NP is home to the Old-Growth Bottomland Forest Research and Education Center, one of 21 centers nationwide?

    ○ Yes   ○ No

---

b) If YES, which of the following trails did you and your personal group walk/canoe/kayak on this visit? Please mark (●) **all that apply.**

○ Cedar Creek Wilderness Canoe Trail   ○ Bluff Trail
○ Elevated Boardwalk Trail   ○ Kingsnake Trail
○ Low Boardwalk Trail   ○ River Trail
○ Oakridge Trail   ○ Sims Trail
○ Weston Lake Loop Trail
○ Other (Please specify)

11. On this visit, in which activities did you and your personal group participate within Congaree NP? Please mark (●) **all that apply.**

○ Citizen Science program
○ Exercising (jogging, rollerblading, etc.)
○ Nature study (other than birdwatching)
○ Ranger-led programs
○ Visiting the visitor center
○ Walking dogs
○ Walking/hiking
○ Backpacking
○ Birdwatching
○ Camping
○ Canoeing/kayaking
○ Fishing
○ Park special event
○ Picnicking
○ Other (Please specify)

12. On this visit, how many vehicles did you and your personal group use to arrive at the park? Please write "0" if you did not arrive by vehicle.

    ___ Number of vehicles

13. a) How long did you and your personal group stay in the Congaree NP **area** (within 1-hour drive of the park)? Please estimate in hours/days as ¼, ½, ¾.

○ Resident of the area ➔ **Go to part b of this question on next page**

    ___ Number of hours **if less than 24 hours**
- OR -
    ___ Number of days **if 24 hours or more**

b) Did you and your personal group notice any scientists, scientific markers, or scientific equipment at work while you were in the park?

○ Yes   ○ No

c) Did you and your personal group – through programs and products – learn about actual results of scientific studies at the park?

○ Yes   ○ No

16. a) Please mark (●) **all** of the information on services and facilities that you or your personal group **used** at Congaree NP during this visit.

b) For only those services and facilities that you or your personal group **used**, please rate their importance to your visit from 1-5.

c) For only those services and facilities that you or your personal group **used**, please rate their quality from 1-5.

b) If used, how important?
1=Not important
2=Somewhat important
3=Moderately important
4=Very important
5=Extremely important

c) If used, what quality?
1=Very poor
2=Poor
3=Average
4=Good
5=Very good

a) Information services/facilities used?
Mark (●)

○ Assistance from park staff
○ Assistance from park volunteers
○ Bulletin boards
○ Junior or Ranger program
○ Park brochure/map
○ Park interpretive pamphlets
○ Park newspaper *Boardwalk Talk*
○ Park website (nps.gov/cong) used before or during visit
○ Ranger-led talks/programs/walks
○ Ranger-guided canoe tours
○ Visitor center bookstore sales items (section, price, etc.)
○ Visitor center videos/films/movies
○ Visitor center exhibits

---

10

17. a) Please mark (●) **all** of the visitor services and facilities that you or your personal group **used** at Congaree NP during this visit.

b) For only those services and facilities that you or your personal group **used**, please rate their importance to your visit from 1-5.

c) For only those services and facilities that you or your personal group **used**, please rate their quality from 1-5.

b) If used, how important?
1=Not important
2=Somewhat important
3=Moderately important
4=Very important
5=Extremely important

c) If used, what quality?
1=Very poor
2=Poor
3=Average
4=Good
5=Very good

a) Visitor services/facilities used?
Mark (●)

○ Access for people with disabilities
○ Backcountry camping
○ Boardwalks
○ Campgrounds
○ Canoe launches
○ Directional signs outside park
○ Park directional signs
○ Parking areas
○ Picnic areas
○ Restrooms
○ Trails

18. On this visit, were you and your personal group part of the following types of organized groups?

a) Commercial guided tour group   ○ Yes   ○ No

b) School/educational group   ○ Yes   ○ No

c) Other (scouts, work, church, etc.)   ○ Yes   ○ No

d) If you were with one of these organized groups, how many people, including yourself, were in this group?

_____ Number of people in organized group

19. a) On this visit, what kind of personal group (not guided tour/school/other organized group) were you with?

- O Alone
- O Friends
- O Family
- O Family and friends
- O Other (Please specify) _____

b) On this visit, how many people were in your personal group, including yourself?

_____ Number of people

20. For you and your personal group on this visit, please provide the following. (If you do not know the answer, leave blank).

	a) Current age	b) U.S. ZIP code or name of country other than U.S.	Number of visits to Congaree NP (including this visit)		Number of visits to other National Parks (including this visit)	
			c) Past 12 months	d) Lifetime	e) Past 12 months	f) Lifetime
Yourself	_____	_____	_____	_____	_____	_____
Member #2	_____	_____	_____	_____	_____	_____
Member #3	_____	_____	_____	_____	_____	_____
Member #4	_____	_____	_____	_____	_____	_____
Member #5	_____	_____	_____	_____	_____	_____
Member #6	_____	_____	_____	_____	_____	_____
Member #7	_____	_____	_____	_____	_____	_____

21. For you only, what is the highest level of education you have completed? Please mark (●) one.

- O Some high school
- O High school diploma/GED
- O Some college
- O Bachelor's degree
- O Graduate degree

22. a) Does anyone in your personal group have mobility or other physical impairments?

- O Yes
- O No → **Go on to Question 23**

b) If YES, did anyone in your personal group have a physical condition that made it difficult to access or participate in park activities or services?

- O Yes
- O No

---

23. a) Are you or members of your personal group Hispanic or Latino? Please mark (●) **one** for each group member.

	Yourself	Member #2	Member #3	Member #4	Member #5	Member #6	Member #7
Yes, Hispanic or Latino	O	O	O	O	O	O	O
No, not Hispanic or Latino	O	O	O	O	O	O	O

b) What is your race? What is the race of each member of your personal group? Please mark (●) **one or more** for you and each group member.

	Yourself	Member #2	Member #3	Member #4	Member #5	Member #6	Member #7
American Indian or Alaska Native	O	O	O	O	O	O	O
Asian	O	O	O	O	O	O	O
Black or African American	O	O	O	O	O	O	O
Native Hawaiian or other Pacific Islander	O	O	O	O	O	O	O
White	O	O	O	O	O	O	O

24. a) On this trip, if you and your personal group had not chosen to visit Congaree NP, what other recreation site would you have visited instead?

_____

b) How far is this alternative site from your home? _____ miles

25. a) Which category best represents your annual **household** income? Please mark (●) **only one.**

- O Less than $24,999
- O $25,000-$34,999
- O $35,000-$49,999
- O $50,000-$74,999
- O $75,000-$99,999
- O $100,000-$149,999
- O $150,000-$199,999
- O $200,000 or more
- O Do not wish to answer

b) How many people are in your household? _____ Number of people

c) Did your household take any unpaid vacation or take unpaid time off of work to come on this trip?

- O Yes
- O No

26. For you and your personal group, please estimate all expenditures for the items listed below for this visit to Congaree NP and the surrounding area (within 1-hour drive of the park). **Please write "0" if no money was spent in a particular category.**

a) Please estimate your personal group's total expenditures inside Congaree NP.

b) Please estimate your personal group's total expenditures in the **surrounding area outside the park** (within 1-hour drive of the park).

> NOTE: Surrounding area residents should only include expenditures that were **just for this trip** to Congaree NP.

EXPENDITURES

	a) Inside park	b) Outside park
Lodges, hotels, motels, cabins, B&B, etc.	n/a	$ _____
Camping fees and charges		$ _____
Canoe/kayak rental charges	n/a	$ _____
Guide fees and charges	n/a	$ _____
Restaurants and bars	n/a	$ _____
Groceries and takeout food	n/a	$ _____
Gas and oil (auto, RV, boat, etc.)	n/a	$ _____
Other transportation expenses (rental cars, taxis, auto repairs, but NOT airfare)	n/a	$ _____
Admission, recreation, entertainment fees	n/a	$ _____
All other purchases (souvenirs, film, books, sporting goods, clothing, etc.)	$ _____	$ _____
Donations	$ _____	$ _____

c) How many people do the above expenses cover?

_____ Adults (18 years or over) _____ Children (under 18 years)

Please write "0" if no children were covered by the expenditures.

27. Overall, how would you rate the quality of the facilities, services, and recreational opportunities provided to you and your personal group at Congaree NP during this visit? Please mark (●) **one.**

Very poor	Poor	Average	Good	Very good
○	○	○	○	○

28. Would you and your group be likely to visit Congaree NP again in the future?

Yes	No	Not sure
○	○	○

29. Please indicate how the following elements may have affected you and your personal group's park experience during this visit to Congaree NP. Please mark (●) **only one** for each element.

Affect your park experience?	Detracted from	No effect	Added to	Did not experience
Airplane noise	○	○	○	○
Automobile noise	○	○	○	○
Gunshots from neighboring lands	○	○	○	○
Noise from park staff activities (such as chainsaws, leaf blowers, generators, etc.)	○	○	○	○
Train noise	○	○	○	○
Other visitors' activities	○	○	○	○
Small number of visitors on trails	○	○	○	○
Large number of visitors on trails	○	○	○	○
Small number of visitors canoeing/kayaking	○	○	○	○
Large number of visitors canoeing/kayaking	○	○	○	○
Impact of wild pigs	○	○	○	○
Other (Please specify)	○	○	○	○

30. If you were to visit Congaree NP in the future, which types of organized activities and programs would you and your personal group like to have available? Please mark (●) **all that apply.**

- ○ Not interested in organized activities/programs → **Go on to Question 31**
- ○ Art/photography
- ○ Bird walks
- ○ Camping (family)
- ○ Camping (educational)
- ○ Canoe/kayaking
- ○ Children's programs
- ○ Family activities
- ○ History tours
- ○ Night walk/night sky program
- ○ Outdoor recreation workshop
- ○ Owl prowls
- ○ Ranger-led programs
- ○ Special events/festivals
- ○ Volunteer opportunities (ways to help the park)
- ○ Other (Please specify) _____

PO 1139

31. If you were to v s t Congaree NP n the future, wh ch subjects wou d you and your
persona group ke to earn about? P ease mark (●) all that app y.

O   Not nterested n earn ng about these subjects → **Go to Question 32**

O   Cha enges fac ng park   O   Natura resource management

O   Champ on trees   O   O d growth f oodp a n forest

O   C mate change   O   P ants/an ma s

O   Current research   O   Threatened/endangered spec es

O   H story   O   Vo unteer opportun t es
                                          (ways to he p the park)

O   Internat ona B osphere Reserve   O   W derness

O   Recreat ona opportun t es (canoe ng/kayak ng, f sh ng, camp ng, etc.)

O   Other (P ease spec fy) _____

32. a) What d d you and your persona group ke **most** about your v s t to Congaree NP?
_____
_____

   b) What d d you and your persona group ke **least** about your v s t to Congaree NP?
_____
_____

33. Congaree NP was estab shed because of ts s gn f cance to the nat on. In your
op n on, what s the nat ona s gn f cance of th s park?
_____
_____

34. If you were a manager p ann ng for the future of Congaree NP what wou d you and
your persona group propose?
_____
_____

35. Is there anyth ng e se you and your persona group wou d ke to te us about your
v s t to Congaree NP?
_____
_____

Thank you for your he p! P ease sea the quest onna re n the postage pa d enve ope
prov ded and drop t n any U.S. ma box.
♻ Printed on recycled paper

Appendix 2: Additional Analysis

The Visitor Services Project (VSP) offers the opportunity to learn from VSP visitor study data through additional analysis. Two-way and three-way cross tabulations can be made with any questions.

Below are some examples of the types of cross tabulations that can be requested. To make a request, please use the contact information below, and include your name, address and phone number in the request.

1. What proportion of family groups with children attends interpretive programs?

2. Is there a correlation between visitors' ages and their preferred sources of information about the park?

3. Are highly satisfied visitors more likely to return for a future visit?

4. How many international visitors participate in hiking?

5. What ages of visitors would use the park website as a source of information on a future visit?

6. Is there a correlation between visitor groups' rating of the overall quality of their park experience and their ratings of individual services and facilities?

7. Do larger visitor groups (e.g., four or more) participate in different activities than smaller groups?

8. Do frequent visitors rate the overall quality of their park experiences differently than less frequent visitors?

The VSP database website (http://vsp.uidaho.edu) allows data searches for comparisons of data from one or more parks.

For more information please contact:

Visitor Services Project, PSU
College of Natural Resources
P.O. Box 441139
University of Idaho
Moscow, ID 83843-1139

Phone: 208-885-2585
Fax: 208-885-4261
Email: lenale@uidaho.edu
Website: http://www.psu.uidaho.edu

Appendix 3: Decision Rules for Checking Nonresponse Bias

There are several methods for checking non-response bias. However, the most common way is to use some demographic indicators to compare respondents and nonrespondents (Dey 1997; Salant and Dillman 1994; Dillman and Carley-Baxter 2000; Dillman, 2007; Stoop 2004). In this study, group type, group size, age of the group member (at least 16 years old) completing the survey, whether the park was the primary reason for being in the area, and respondent's place of residence were five variables that were used to check for nonresponse bias.

Two independent-sample T-tests were used to test the differences between respondents and nonrespondents. The p-values represent the significance levels of these tests. If the p-value is greater than 0.05, the two groups are judged to be insignificantly different.

Chi-square tests were used to detect the differences in group types, whether the park was the primary reason for being in the area, and respondent's place of residence. The hypotheses were that there would be no significant difference between respondents and nonrespondents in terms of who they travelled with, why they were in the area, or where they came from. If the p-value is greater than 0.05, the differences are judged to be insignificant.

The hypotheses for checking non-response bias are: Respondents and nonrespondents are not significantly difference in terms of:

1. Average age
2. Number of people they were travelling with in a personal group
3. Type of group which they were travelling with
4. How park fit into travel plans
5. Proximity from home to the park

As shown in Tables 3-6, respondents and nonrespondents were not significantly different in terms of group size and primary reason for travelling to the area. The p-values for respondent/nonrespondent average age, group type, and proximity from home to the park are less than 0.05, indicating significant differences between respondents and nonrespondents. The results indicated younger respondents (under 40 years old) may be underrepresented. Visitors who lived within 51 to 100 miles of the park, and visitors who travelled in friends groups may also be underrepresented in the results.

References

Dey, E. L. (1997). Working with Low Survey Response Rates: The Efficacy of Weighting Adjustment. *Research in Higher Education*, 38(2): 215-227.

Dillman, D. A. (2007). *Mail and Internet Surveys: The Tailored Design Method, Updated version with New Internet, Visual, and Mixed-Mode Guide*, 2nd Edition, New York: John Wiley and Sons, Inc.

Dillman, D. A. and Carley-Baxter, L. R. (2000). *Structural determinants of survey response rate over a 12-year period, 1988-1999*, Proceedings of the section on survey research methods, 394-399, American Statistical Association, Washington, DC.

Filion, F. L. (Winter 1975-Winter 1976). Estimating Bias due to Non-response in Mail Surveys. *Public Opinion Quarterly*, Vol 39 (4): 482-492.

Goudy, W. J. (1976). Non-response Effect on Relationships Between Variables. *Public Opinion Quarterly*. Vol 40 (3): 360-369.

Mayer, C. S. and Pratt Jr. R. W. (Winter 1966-Winter 1967). A Note on Non-response in a Mail Survey. *Public Opinion Quarterly*. Vol 30 (4): 637-646.

Salant, P. and Dillman, D. A. (1994). *How to Conduct Your Own Survey*. U.S.: John Wiley and Sons, Inc.

Stoop, I. A. L. (2004). Surveying Non-respondents. *Field Methods*, 16 (1): 23.

NPS 178/119309, December 2012